Making
FABULOUS
SCRAPBOOK PAGES

Are you a scrapbook addict? Welcome to the club—so are we! The papers, the toys, the new techniques…we love just about everything that has to do with scrapbooking! In fact, we've been scrapping for more than seven years, ever since we came out with a line of patterned paper called Paper Pizazz™. (You might have heard of it—hey, you might have even started scrapbooking with Paper Pizazz™!)

But we're growing up. We're changing. And if you've read our other scrapbooking idea books (like *Making Marvelous Scrapbook Pages*), you'll notice that *Making Fabulous* is a little different.

First, the layouts in this book have a more sophisticated style—coordinating subtly patterned papers, placing just a few photos on a page and adding a few embellishments as a special touch. You'll also see a different layout throughout this book: selected album pages are given a full page to themselves. We've done this so you can more easily see the details of each technique. It's almost like holding the page in your hand!

In addition, we're delighted to welcome two very talented new designers to our team of Scrapbook Specialists: Paris Dukes and Toddi Barclay debut their unique styles in *Making Fabulous Scrapbook Pages*. And we're thrilled to present the winning style of our online contest winners, Lisa LaCentra, Allison Macdonald and Kimberly Llorens. (Enter on our website, www.paperpizazz.com) and you may find your page in the next idea book!)

Our goal is to bring the newest, most exciting techniques to our favorite scrapbookers—you! We're glad to be scrapping, growing and changing right along with you.

Thanks to our talented page designers. In alphabetical order, they are:
- **Toddi Barclay** for Hot Off The Press, Inc.
- **Shauna Berglund-Immel** for Hot Off The Press, Inc.
- **Susan Cobb** for Hot Off The Press, Inc.
- **Natalie Dukes,** Hillsboro, Oregon
- **Paris Dukes** for Hot Off The Press, Inc.
- **Lisa Garcia-Bergstedt,** Portland, Oregon
- **LeNae Gerig** for Hot Off The Press, Inc.
- **Spencer Immel,** Beaverton, Oregon
- § **Lisa La Centra,** Portland, Oregon
- § **Kimberly Llorens,** Portland, Oregon
- § **Allison Macdonald,** Arlington, Texas
- **Sara Naumann** for Hot Off The Press, Inc.
- **Arlene Peterson** for Hot Off The Press, Inc.

§ *contest winner!*

Production Credits:
- **President:** Paulette Jarvey
- **Vice-President:** Teresa Nelson
- **Production Manager:** Lynda Hill
- **Editors:** Paulette Jarvey, Lynda Hill
- **Project Editors:** Sherry Harbert, India de Kanter
- **Photographer:** John McNally
- **Graphic Designers:** Jacie Pete, Joy Schaber
- **Digital Imagers:** Victoria Weber, Scott Gordon

published by:

HOT OFF THE PRESS INC.

©2003 by **HOT OFF THE PRESS** INC. All rights reserved. No part of this publication may be reproduced in any form or by any means, including photocopying, without permission in writing from the publisher. Printed in the United States of America.

Hot Off The Press wants to be kind to the environment. Whenever possible we follow the 3 R's—reduce, reuse and recycle. We use soy and UV inks that greatly reduce the release of volatile organic solvents.

For a color catalog of nearly 800 products, send $2.00 to:

HOT OFF THE PRESS INC.
1250 N.W. Third, Dept. B
Canby, Oregon 97013
phone (503) 266-9102
fax (503) 266-8749
www.paperpizazz.com

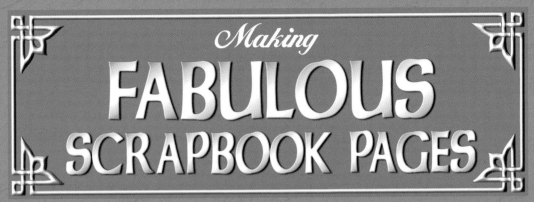

Making
FABULOUS
SCRAPBOOK PAGES

It's Easier Than You Think

Includes:

- 168 scrapbook pages
- contest winners
- 15 mini-classes
- masculine pages & lumpy layouts
- heartfelt journaling
- metal embossing & more!

From the creators of:

- *Making Great Scrapbook Pages*
- *Making Terrific Scrapbook Pages*
- *Making Marvelous Scrapbook Pages*

Table of Contents

6
Design Elements
Ideas, tips and tricks for making your pages the best they can be!

16
Designer Pages
See what happens when different scrapbook designers use the same photos or papers or even layouts

38
You Asked For It
We're giving it to you— masculine, tags, stickers and vellum ideas!

56
3-D & Lumpy Pages
Add a dash of dimension to your pages with these ideas!

68
Heartfelt Journaling
Pour your heart onto the page!

76
Mini Classes
Learn cutting-edge techniques to make your pages look fabulous!

124
Coordinating 2-page Spreads
If one is good—two is better! We show you how, here.

130
Gift Albums
We wrap it up with spectacular ways to present your pages inside albums. What a great finish!

Overlap
Elements

Vary the
Photo Size

Play Time Fun
Hailey
May 2002

Time
with my
family
is the
most
special
time
of all.

June
2002

Gone
Fishing

Fill the
Center

My favorite time with dad
is when we go fishing. It is
our special time to just
hang out and be together.

Jack and Dad
September 2002

Establish a
Focal Point

Vary the
Photo Shape

Dad
&
Jake

June
2002

Sydney & Brendan
October 2002

Follow the
"Golden Rule"

Design Elements

You've got the photos. You've picked out your papers. You've journaled. You've selected tags, eyelets, fibers and buttons to accent your page. But after you lay everything out, you discover there's something that's just not quite right.

Is it the photo? The paper? The journaling? Or maybe you didn't pick the right tag or fiber? No—the answer doesn't have anything to do with the elements of your page. Rather, it has to do with Design Elements.

Sounds technical, doesn't it? It's really not. In fact, "Design Elements" are just design guidelines used to lay out the pieces (photos, journaling and embellishments) that make up a page. These guidelines are the foundation for choosing papers, selecting embellishments and laying out your page. Learn them and you'll have tools for taking better photos, simple ways to make those photos stand out on a page, and how to place your elements to turn a so-so layout into a great one.

Professional scrapbook designers know these Design Elements well, and our Scrapbook Specialists are no exception. Turn the page to learn the tools of Design Elements!

Sometimes posed, often spontaneous—a photo captures a moment of time. Use the camera as an extension of your eye to catch your perception of the occasion. You'll add more fun and interest to your pages.

Living involves many emotions. Don't shoot only happy faces. Capture all of life!

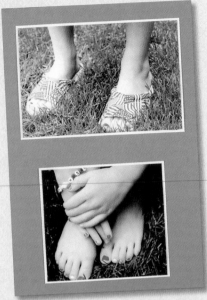

Not a face anywhere but these shots tell a wonderfully tender story. Shooting extreme close-ups provide a uniquely personal perspective.

Tilting the camera adds a light-hearted touch a photo such as the fun spirit displayed by this young rider.

Shooting up or shooting down gives a new perspective. It can also produce some great "fun house" effects.

Shoot black & white film occasionally. Study the importance of light and shadow. Try using it for a different effect.

To crop: Trim close to the focal person, place or thing. Use straight or pattern-edged scissors. For smooth ovals, perfect circles and great shapes use a plastic template. Place the template on top of the photo and draw the shape on the photo with a pencil, then cut just inside the line. Lots of shapes are available.

Leave historical items like houses, cars, or furniture—they'll be fun to see years from now.

If you're hesitant about cropping older or one-of-a-kind photos, make a color copy (yes, a color copy is best even for black-and-white photos) and cut the copy for your album page.

To mat: Glue your cropped photo to a sheet of paper and cut $1/8"$–$1/2"$ away, forming a mat. Use plain paper for the first mat (see the Golden Rule on page 13). Use straight or pattern-edge scissors. Double and triple mat some photos.

Color blocking with mats adds dimension and can help call attention to a special photo.

Tearing the mat (see page 11) can add texture to a page.

Offset matting is a great way to emphasize a photo. Use different vellum colors as shown for dramatic mats!

Design Elements: Tools & Techniques

The right tools can make all the difference. We've gathered the tools we think are the most effective and included a few tips on how to use them. We want your scrapbooking experience to be fun and enjoyable—now get scrapping!

Eyelets & Snaps:

Eyelet setter and bit set.

From left: Handheld hole punch, hammer, anywhere hole punch, eyelet setter.

1 From the front of the paper, punch a hole with the anywhere hole punch. Then insert the eyelet or snap.

2 From the back of the paper, use the hammer and setter to pound down the edge to secure the eyelet or snap.

Brads:

1 Punch a hole. Cut a slit or use a tack (for tiny holes) where you want the brad to be.

2 Insert the brad extensions through the paper from the front.

3 Open the extensions from the back of the paper to secure.

Glues for Lumpy Items:

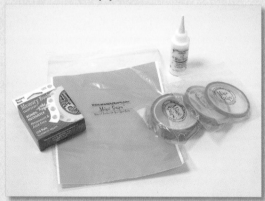

Clockwise, from left: adhesive Glue Dots™, Scrappy Tape sheets, Scrappy Glue and Scrappy Tape rolls (also known as Terrifically Tacky Tape).

Embossing on Metal:

From left: foam mouse pad, templates, wood stylus and tracing wheel.

Use a mouse pad to cushion the metal as you emboss.

Chalking:

Chalk tools from left, sponge applicator, cosmetic sponge, cotton swab and Pazzles clamp with pom pom. Use your favorite!

Apply chalk to the edges of torn paper or torn vellum to add depth.

Or use it to shade die-cuts and Cut-Outs™.

Tearing Paper:

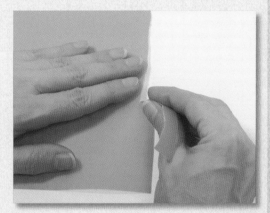

Pulling the paper towards you while tearing creates a white edge.

Tear the paper away from you for a colored edge. Use your fingers for controlled tearing.

Tear vellum with the grain of the paper for a smooth edge.

Tieing Lumpy Fibers:

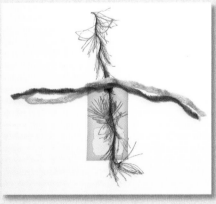

1 Thread a thin fiber through the hole or eyelet.

2 Lay the lumpy fibers across the thin fiber.

3 Tie the thin fiber around the lumpy fibers.

4 Tie the lumpy fibers together. Yahoo!

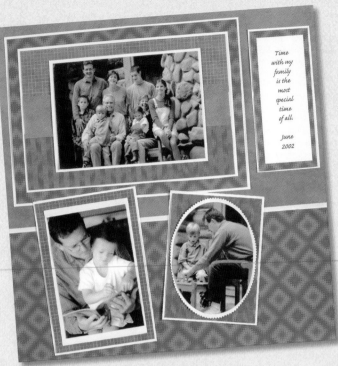

#1 Establish a focal point:

The "focal point" is the element on an album page which first attracts the eye. A page without a clear focal point lacks interest. One way to create a focal point is to enlarge the main photo and add a large mat—as Arlene did with the top photo.

- **patterned Paper Pizazz™:** blue diamond, purple/blue stripes, purple grid, blue sponged (*Mixing Masculine*)
- **solid Paper Pizazz™:** white (*Plain Pastels*)
- **mini-pinking pattern edge scissors:** Fiskars®
- **designer:** Arlene Peterson

#2 Vary the photo sizes:

Having one photo clearly larger than the rest adds interest to your page. Arlene balanced the large photo with borders on the right hand side of the page and oversized journaling at the bottom.

- **patterned Paper Pizazz™:** multi-colored posies on white, multi-colored posies on purple, purple scuffed (*Mixing Baby*)
- **vellum Paper Pizazz™:** pale purple (*12"x12" Pastel Vellum Papers*, also by the sheet)
- **solid Paper Pizazz™:** white (*Plain Pastel Papers*)
- **designer:** Arlene Peterson

#3 Vary the photo shapes:

All rectangles (or all circles or even all hearts) may lead to a bland page. Change the shape of one or two photos or other elements to provide variety and keep the eye moving around the page.

- **patterned Paper Pizazz™:** blue grid, blue triangles, blue hollow dot (*12"x12" Jewel Tints*)
- **solid Paper Pizazz™:** white (*Plain Pastels*), navy blue (*Solid Jewel Tones*)
- **sailboat cut-out:** Paper Pizazz™ *Vellum Cut-Outs™ #2*
- **designer:** Arlene Peterson

#4

Overlapping elements: Wonderful things happen when page elements touch and overlap! Not only is the viewer's eye directed from one element to another in a clear path but you can fit more or larger pieces on the page.

- **patterned Paper Pizazz™:** light blue floral, dark blue floral (*Flowered "Handmade" Papers*)
- **specialty Paper Pizazz™:** metallic gold (*Metallic Gold,* also by the sheet), pale blue vellum (*12"x12" Pastel Vellum Papers,* also by the sheet)
- **Paper Pizazz™ Cut-Outs™:** blue wedding bells, doves, bells pocket (*Vellum Envelopes and Pockets*)
- **designer:** Arlene Peterson

#5

Fill the center: Your eye is naturally drawn to the center of a page; if it's empty, the page looks incomplete. The vellum strips and the dangling fish give the eye a place to rest.

- **patterned Paper Pizazz™:** green swirl, green marble (*Great Jewel Backgrounds*)
- **vellum Paper Pizazz™:** pastel green (*12"x12" Pastel Vellum Papers,* also by the sheet), white (*Vellum Papers,* also by the sheet)
- **solid Paper Pizazz™:** black (*Solid Jewel Tones*)
- **fish, sign:** Paper Pizazz™ *Vellum #2 Cut-Outs™*
- **jute twine:** Darice, Inc.
- **designer:** Arlene Peterson

#6

Follow **"The Golden Rule"** for patterned papers. **Mat your photos on plain paper before placing them on patterned backgrounds.** A plain mat visually separates the photo from a patterned background and helps it pop off the page. On this page, the solid mats give the eye relief from the patterned papers.

- **patterned Paper Pizazz™:** leaf, stripes (*Joy's Garden*)
- **solid Paper Pizazz™:** light orange, dark orange, light green, dark green (*Muted Tints*)
- **leaves:** Paper Pizazz™ *Vellum Cut-Outs™ #2*
- **designer:** Arlene Peterson

So many colors and patterns and all so beautiful! How do you choose? It's easy with these simple guidelines. Each begins with the photo.

Match the Clothing Colors

1 A darling princess and a sparkly tiara made choosing papers easy! The blue metallic papers to coordinate with Elise's t-shirt. Gems, glitter and beads echo the tiara and the writing on the t-shirt. This page twinkles and shines—perfect papers for a pretty princess. See page 52 for complete instructions and materials.

2 A handsome page for a handsome man! Rick's navy blue shirt pulls the dark blue from the plaid background. The stripes, gingham and lines papers compliment and coordinate with the photo and emphasize the blue. See page 119 for complete instructions and materials.

Match the Photo Background

1 Beautiful rhododenrons inspired this pretty page! The lavender companion papers—plaid and floral—pull the color from the background of the photo and onto the page. The coordinating purple floral tag, purple fibers with silver brads and eyelets bring all the elements together. See page 74 for complete instructions and materials.

2 Everybody loves a bubble bath! Bubbles background paper captures the setting of the page. The blue swirl paper is reminiscent of water and fits the mood perfectly. See page 47 for complete instructions and materials.

Match the Photo Theme

1 Fishing is a classic pastime and these papers fit the theme perfectly! A fishing collage page is a background and vellum fish tags continue the theme. Solid matting papers emphasize the photo and follow the "Golden Rule." See page 47 for complete instructions and materials.

2 Indepence day memories are perfect for America's colors—red, white and blue! Flag with white stars on navy papers carry out the theme of the photo. White and navy paper are perfect for simple matting effects, and vellum is great for journaling and accents. This bold page is filled with pride! See page 70 for complete instructions and materials.

We created this patriotic sample page in seven easy steps! Remember that there is no "wrong" way to build a page—the best pages come from the heart.

#2 Select your papers— plain, patterned and accent, such as *Tag Art*, to complement your photos. See pages 14-15 for more tips.

#1 Select your photos based on the theme or event for your album page. You might think of each scrapbook page as having a story to tell.

#3 Crop and mat your photos (see page 10). Try enlarging or shrinking the photos on a color copier for different effects.

#4 Journal on the computer or by hand, then trim the paper to fit your page layout. This is where you add the words to finish your page's story. Keep it brief or make it as complete as you think necessary.

#6 Create a tag—or add stickers, buttons, ribbons, etc.—to add dimention and texture to your page.

#5 Arrange the photos and other elements on the background paper without attaching them. This is the time to play with different layouts.

#7 Attach all of your elements and Voila!— the completed page!

Designer Pages

Imagine: A room filled with papers, vellum, embellishments. Now imagine calling this room your office. Well, our Scrapbook Specialists do. For these women, the daily 9-5 means paper, scissors and glue—and a whole lot more. It sounds like a blast—and it is— but it's also hard work. After all, these professional designers create hundreds of fantastic, technique-based album pages each year. And there's always a deadline!

The Scrapbook Specialists have a very important responsibility: To create album pages that inspire and delight one very important person—you! Their job is to dream up new techniques and design new layouts so YOU can be a better scrapbooker. It's a lot of responsibility, but these talented women are definitely up to the challenge.

In this chapter, you'll meet a few of the Scrapbook Specialists. You'll see their diverse scrapbooking styles, and their individual talents. They'll teach you how to create different looks from a single layout, and how to scrapbook the same set of photos three different ways. They'll even divulge a few of their secrets so you can be a Scrapbook Specialist too!

Come play with us—come scrapbook with the Specialists!

Arlene is a Technical Editor, Scrapbook Specialist and teaches scrapbooking classes across the United States. She lives in Oregon with her huband, Craig, their youngest daughter, Missy, and their two dogs, Kookie and Nike. In her spare time she enjoys crafting of every kind. Thanks, Arlene, for all of your hard work and beautiful pages!

Tips from Arlene Peterson

GET A NEW PERSPECTIVE: Do you scrapbook sitting down? Then stand up to get a different perspective and move your photos around to test different combinations. If you stand while you scrapbook, try putting your page on the floor. If you have scrapper's block, arrange your photos and other elements on the background paper but don't glue them down. Then walk away—come back in a few minutes and see how the arrangement strikes you. Sometimes you'll be able to spot a problem area right away and other times you'll find your first reaction is, "Hey, that looks great!"

PRINTING ON VELLUM: (1) Go into your printer set-up and adjust it to the Transparency setting. This will put the least amount onto the vellum. **(2)** Go into page set-up in your word processing program and set the margin 1" from the top of the page. This will allow the printer time to get a "hold" on the vellum and reduces smearing. And yes, you can cut a 12"x12" sheet of vellum to 8½"x11" and put it through a laser printer.

KEEP YOUR CAMERA WITH YOU: Arlene jokes, "I am always taking photos; sometimes my family wonders if it's an extension of my arm!" By keeping her camera close at hand, Arlene is able to capture those everyday moments or spontaneous activities. "Don't skimp on film—take at least three photos of each event, occasion or setting. Some will turn out better than others. Try shooting the same scene from a couple of different angles to get the best variety," Arlene advises. Most importantly, Arlene reminds us to have plenty of photos taken of yourself—you are, after all, a pretty important part of the memory!

EMOBSSING ON METAL: Place the metal on a piece of craft foam (available at your local craft store) or a mouse pad. This will cushion the metal, which is especially important when using a tracing wheel.

WORKING WITH FIBERS: Arlene is a talented seamstress as well as a scrapbooker. She often uses fibers and threads on her pages. Here's what she's learned:

- Floss or jute knots will come loose over time. Put a dab of glue or a Glue Dot™ on the backside of the knot to keep it secure.

- When threading fibers through eyelets, Arlene suggests putting a dab of glue on the end of the fiber length then roll it in your fingers to create one secure end. "It's easier to thread one length of fiber than several!" Arlene says.

- Take the time to mark your stitches on the back of the paper with a pencil before poking holes—it will save you from uneven lines, irregular spacing and wayward holes.

PAPER GRAIN: Many people don't know that paper and vellum have a grain. You'll notice it when tearing paper and vellum—you'll tear a much straighter line when you tear with the grain and a more ragged, uneven edge when you tear against the grain. Try it, you'll see!

Tips from Susan Cobb

WARM AND COOL COLORS: When combining colors, Susan's advise is: Stay warm or stay cool. "Combining colors in the same tones is virtually foolproof," she says. "It's the perfect method for a subtle, sophisticated layout."

- **Warm** colors include red, orange, peach and yellow. While **cool** colors are those like blue, purple and teal. **Neutrals** are colors that don't compete with other colors: white, off-white, grey, black and beige. Neutrals can also be warm or cool. For example, white looks great with other cool colors like blue. While off-white looks better with a warm orange. The same is true for metallics: silver is cool and gold, bronze or copper are warm.

- **Complimentary colors** are those across from each other on the color wheel. They are opposite: red and green, yellow and purple, blue and orange. "These color combinations are interesting—put them together and the result is incredible energy," says Susan. "They're attention-getting, so if your page is high-engergy, these are the colors to combine."

APPLYING GLITTER: Susan uses Magic Scraps Scrappy Glue to apply glitter in a fine line. She advises practising first on scrap paper to get the right amount of pressure for the line size you need. If you want an ultra-thin line, run an X-acto® knife along the edge of the glue line to make it even thinner. Then add the glitter.

LAYERING VELLUM: "There are a few tricks to keep in mind when layering vellum," Susan recommends. "Don't layer complimentary colors— if you place green vellum on top of a red background paper, you'll get a murky effect." Susan says mixing tone-on-tone vellums and papers is the easiest way to achieve a great look. "Tone-on-tone" simply means one color paired with a lighter or darker color in the same family—light green and dark green, for example. "Placing a light blue patterned vellum over a paper in another shade of blue will give you extra dimension," she says.

DISTRESSING BUTTONS: Sand painted buttons for a distressed effect. "I use Magic Scraps buttons, which are plastic with a painted surface that can be sanded off. Buttons that are just plastic will be the same color throughout the button, and the technique won't work." It doesn't take much pressure to get the effect—do a little at a time, checking frequently to make sure you don't over do it. Use a mini Glue Dot™ to hold the button to your work surface while sanding. See the Mini Class on distressing starting on page 112.

FOLDING FRAMES: When folding paper or vellum frames, it's easy to adjust the size to fit your photograph. To increase the size, start with a larger square *of the same proportion as the original*. This will result in a larger frame with a similar look and will be folded in the same way as the original. Use the same method to decrease the size. See the Mini Class on folded frames starting on page 108.

Susan is a Technical Editor, Scrapbook Specialist and an incredible paper engineer. In her spare time she enjoys drawing and painting. Susan lives in Oregon with her husband, Brian, their two daughters and two cats. We thank her for her wonderful pages and dedication!

Tips from Shauna Berglund-Immel

SUPER STITCHING: Shauna suggests this shortcut for stitching on a layout: Use a needle, the tip of an X-acto® knife or an awl to pre-prick the holes. You can use a ruler to make sure they're equidistant and in a straight line. When it comes to sewing, it's much easier to just follow the guide you've made, and you don't hurt your fingers trying to jam the needle through the paper!

PLAY WITH PHOTOS: Take advantage of color copies and Kodak Picture Makers to enlarge or shrink your photographs. You can also change color photos to black and white. "I like to do this when the colors in the photos don't match the papers I want to use. It's an easy way to solve the problem of your daughter being dressed in orange for Christmas pictures!" says Shauna.

SCRAP IN A "Z" FORMATION: Did you know eye "reads" a scrapbook page the same way it does a book? The eye starts "reading" the page at the top left corner, travels to the top right, then diagonally across the center of the page to the bottom left corner. An easy-to-read layout will have an element in each of these hotspots for the reader's eye to rest upon.

TEARING TIPS: Tear vellum and paper towards you to get a white edge, tear away for a colored edge. The white edge provides a mat or visual space. This allows you to place a torn strip of patterned paper onto a patterned background without the two patterns competing. White edges can also be chalked for a pretty tone-on-tone effect.

Shauna is a Scrapbook Specialist who loves lumpy pages. She lives in Oregon with her husband, Dave, and their two children, Spencer and Kaelin. In her spare time she collects children's books and loves sports. Thanks, Shauna, for your fabulous pages!

Tips from Paris Dukes

PRESERVING NEWSPAPER CLIPPINGS: Want to scrapbook magazine or newspaper clippings? Newsprint contains lignin, so you don't want to place the clipping in your scrapbook. "My suggestion is to make a color copy of the article onto acid-free, lignin-free paper," say Paris. The front page of a standard newspaper typically measures a bit larger than 11"x13," while most of our scrapbooks are a standard 8½"x11" or 12"x12". Can you reduce the size without losing the readability? If not, consider making a pocket page by cutting a sheet of paper in half horizontally and attaching three sides to the background paper. Fold the copy and tuck it inside the pocket.

FABULOUS FOIL EMBELLISHMENTS: Love the look of metal foil embellishments? Make your own, customized to match your page—run metal foil through a die-cut machine or use punches to create personalized page accents.

MAKE A TWO-ON-ONE MAT: Paris' no-fail scrapping shortcut: "I love matting two photos together onto the same piece of solid paper. This saves a lot of time and looks great!"

ADHERING MICRO BEADS: Magic Scraps Scrappy Glue or Scappy Tape are great for adhering micro beads. The adhesive dries clear so the paper color will show through the clear beads on top. The tape is perfect for making beaded borders or creating accents with straight edges.

ATTACHING LUMPY EMBELLISHMENTS: "I use Glue Dots™ to adhere charms, fibers, ribbons, buttons and other three-dimensional embellishments to a page," says Paris. Place the Glue Dot™ directly on your embellishment—don't try to transfer the super-sticky dot with your finger—then stick the embellishment to the page.

Paris is a Scrapbook Specialist and especially loves paper piecing. She lives in Oregon with her husband, Jim, and their daughter, Natalie. In her spare time she loves to bake, cook and travel. Thanks, Paris, for your glorious pages and super sharp scissors!

Tips from Toddi Barclay

PAPER SCRAP TIPS: Most scrappers (and card makers) follow the Paper Scrap Rule: If the scrap is the width of a pencil or larger, by all means save it—you never know when you'll need a ⅛" wide piece of pale blue paper, right? Now that you have these scraps, what can you do with them? Make paper knots (glue two strips together back to back for strength), weave long strips together for a border, make a mosaic accent or create a bargello design. Store paper scraps by color in plastic storage bags to keep them organized.

SCRAP WITH FEWER PHOTOS: "I used to think I had to use every picture I took," says Toddi. "Then I realized my layouts actually looked a lot better when I chose just the best photos of the occasion. Often that is one or two photos per scrapbook page." Fewer photos allow for a cleaner, simpler look—the others can be used for gift albums, special theme albums, etc.

STORING UN-SCRAPPED PHOTOS: If you're like most of us, you've got photos that aren't anywhere *near* being scrapbooked. Careful storeage for your un-scrapbooked photos is important too. Two great options are photo boxes and 3-ring binders with photo sleeves. Photo boxes are just the right size for photos, and have plastic or paper dividers to keep them organized. 3-ring binders with photo sleeves allow you to view your photos, even display them, until you scrapbook them.

USING "OOPS" PHOTOS: Save those less-than-stellar photos. Extra shots of grass, flowers and other backgrounds are perfect for punching, creating mosaics, die-cut letters and weaving! "I've found that having lots of options for using extra photos makes it easier to select the best pictures to go in my "big" family album," say Toddi. "I don't stress out about wasting photos since I know I can use all of them for one project or another."

Toddi is the newest member of the Hot Off The Press design team. She is a Scrapbook Specialist and collage fanatic. She lives in Washington with her husband, Brian, and their dog, Pete. In her spare time she enjoys exploring the Pacific Northwest wonderland. Thanks, Toddi, for your fantastic contributions!

LeNae is a Scrapbook Specialist and our in-house craft expert. She lives in Oregon with her husband, Chris, their daughter, Lauren, and their dog, Bailey. In her spare time she likes to explore new craft and search for antiques. Thanks, LeNae, for your fabulous work and many ideas!

Tips from LeNae Gerig

GORGEOUS HANDWRITING THE EASY WAY: For perfect handwriting on vellum use a computer. Computer journal onto scrap paper, then trace it onto vellum with markers or gel pens. Or computer journal directly onto vellum—both plain and patterned vellum work wonderfully. Let the ink dry completely before you cut or handle it.

FACE SUBJECTS INTO THE PAGE: A general graphic design guideline is to make sure your subjects are facing into the page. The people in your photo should be facing into the center of your album and all embellishments should "point" in that direction as well. For example, place a car Punch-Out™ so that it is "driving" toward the center of the page. Doing otherwise will lead the viewer's eye right off the page!

COMPUTER JOURNALING: For picture-perfect journaling, LeNae relies on her computer. Computer journaling gives LeNae a variety of fonts to choose from, plus access to spell-check and even a thesaurus for creative inspiration. She's even found she writes more detail with computer journaling. "I can make sure it's exactly what I want before I print it out," she says.

Quadrant pages can take many forms. How can these three pages look so different, yet be based on the same design? Each page has been divided into four sections. Each page contains two photos that overlap quadrants, either the photo or the matting. Each page has "page corners" and a horizontal element across the center. The similarities may be subtle, but that just illustrates how versatile this format truly is. Here are three takes on this classic design…

#1 **Sentiments can by expressed in many forms, and Paris chose soft and subtle papers for this page.**

1 Paris cut four 5¼" squares from the companion collage papers that included a word in each. She matted them on silver and placed them on solid pastel purple background paper.

5 Paris computer journaled on vellum, cut it to 4¾"x3¼" and added eyelet words to the journaling. She cut a 13" length of satin ribbon, strung three beads and placed it over the vellum. Layers and beads add to the depth and texture of this pretty page.

2 The "page corners" are made of ribbon. Paris wrapped the top left corner with two 6" lengths of ribbon, one sheer and one satin strung with three beads. On the remaining corners she wrapped each with two 2½" lengths of ribbon, one sheer and one satin strung with one bead.

4 Paris cut a 5⅛"x7½" of vellum and placed the photo on the top half. She cut a 4¾"x3¼" of collage paper around "hope" and placed it on the bottom half of the vellum. She copied the photo and punched out the faces.

3 Paris wrapped two 13" lengths of sheer ribbon between the squares, crossing them in the center using one for the horizontal element.

- **patterned Paper Pizazz™:** purple words collage companion papers (*Jacie's Collage*)
- **specialty Paper Pizazz™:** pastel purple vellum (*12"x12" Pastel Vellum Papers,* also by the sheet), metallic silver (*Metallic Silver,* also by the sheet)
- **solid Paper Pizazz™:** pastel purple (*12"x12" Solid Pastel Papers*)
- **silver beads:** Blue Moon Beads/Elizabeth Ward & Co., Inc.

- **⅝" wide sheer lavender ribbon:** C.M. Offray & Son, Inc.
- **⅛" wide lavender satin ribbon:** Sheer Creations
- **eyelet words:** Making Memories™ Details™
- **1¾" square punch:** Marvy® Uchida
- **black pen:** Zebra Jimnie Gel Rollerball
- **adhesive dots:** Glue Dots™
- **designer:** Paris Dukes

#2 This festive page was built with companion holiday papers. Toddi cut a 6" square from blue dots & lines and one from diamond dots. She matted the squares on black then placed them in opposite corners of the blue quilt background paper. She easily created the quadrant just by cutting the two squares! For the "page corners" Toddi cut four 2" squares of red plaid paper and matted each on black. She then cut two 1" squares blue diamond and two from dots & lines. For the center of each corner she punched ½" snowflakes from red plaid and black. Toddi triple-matted each photo on black, red plaid and black again. For the horizontal element Toddi chose three snowflake motifs. She used the die-cut for the large snowflakes—she ghosted the dots & lines and diamond dots papers by layering vellum over them. She punched one ½" snowflake from diamond dots, two from red plaid and three from black. Toddi also punched 1½" snowflakes— three from black, one from dots & lines, one from red plaid and one from diamond dots. What an interesting take on a quadrant page!

- **patterned Paper Pizazz™**: snow on red plaid, blue quilt, blue dots & lines, diamond dots (*Mixing Christmas Papers*)
- **vellum Paper Pizazz™**: white (*Vellum Papers*, also by the sheet)
- **solid Paper Pizazz™**: black (*Solid Jewel Tones*)
- **#3 snowflake die-cut**: Accu/Cut® Systems
- **½", 1½" snowflake punches**: Marvy® Uchida
- **black pen**: Sakura of America
- **designer**: Toddi Barclay

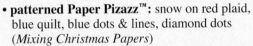

#3 Petit quadrants for petit little girls on a pink buds background sheet! Susan cut eight 4½" squares, two from pink X's, two from pink vellum, two from flower vellum and two from white. She layered a flowers vellum square on each pink X, and matted them on pink then silver. She placed one in the top left and one in the bottom right corners. She placed the pink vellum in the remaining corners. Susan cut two 2" pink X's squares, matted them on silver and centered them on the pink vellums. She cut two single flowers from the flowers vellum and placed them on the pink X's. The "page corners" are two 2" squares of vellum, one pink and one flowers. Susan cut each in half diagonally and placed them in the corners. For the horizontal element Susan cut an 11¾"x1" pink vellum strip and overlayed it on an 11¾"x2" flower vellum strip. She matted each photo on pink and silver then placed them off center on the page. Susan polished the page with black journaling and silver outlines on the vellums.

metallic silver (*Metallic Silver*, also by the sheet)
- **solid Paper Pizazz™**: white, pale pink (*Plain Pastels*)
- **black pen**: Zig® Millenium
- **silver pen**: Sakura Gelly Roll
- **designer**: Susan Cobb

- **patterned Paper Pizazz™**: pink buds, pink X's, pink flowers vellum (*Joy's Garden*)
- **specialty Paper Pizazz™**: pale pink vellum (*12"x12" Pastel Vellum Papers*, also by the sheet),

A split background and a large center mat are what these three pages have in common. It's amazing how versatile this layout can be. Let your pages reflect your memories and each page will be perfect. Remember, there is no "wrong" way to dress a page.

#1 A beautiful wedding day reflected with beautiful papers.

1 Susan overlayed a 5"x12" piece of vellum on the blue stripe background.

2 For the large center mat she cut a 10" square of blue flowers and matted it on silver.

6 Silver journaling and penwork bring all the silver elements together to make the page sparkle.

3 She triple-matted the photos on white, silver and vellum.

I'll always love you

Our Wedding Day
April 20, 2002

5 She used the template to cut nested shapes from vellum, blue flowers and silver. She layered them together with foam tape and placed pearls in the center of each.

4 Susan created the pocket out of two 6"x8" pieces of vellum (see pattern on page 143) and added ⅛" wide silver strips. She computer journaled on white paper, cut it to 2¾"x 2½" and matted it on silver.

- **patterned Paper Pizzaz™:** blue flowers, blue stripe (*Jacie's Watercolor Naturals*)
- **specialty Paper Pizzaz™:** pastel blue vellum (*12"x12" Pastel Vellum Papers,* also by the sheet), metallic silver (*Metallic Silver,* also by the sheet)
- **solid Paper Pizzaz™:** white (*Plain Pastels*)
- **Paper Flair™ Nested Shapes template**
- **white fused pearls:** Magic Scraps
- **silver pen:** Sakura Gelly Roll
- **adhesive glue dots:** Glue Dots™
- **adhesive foam tape:** Therm O Web
- **designer:** Susan Cobb

#2 Historical landmarks look right at home on this page! Toddi overlayed a 6"x12" piece of vellum over the crackle background and secured it with brads. For the large center mat she cut a 10" square of cobblestone. Paris triple-matted each photo on brown, cream and vellum then used brads to secure them to the page. She journaled with the black pen on vellum carefully matching the cobblestones. She also cut the vellum to match the cobblestones. More brads and gold charms tie the page together. What a clever way to remember a great vacation!

• **patterned Paper Pizazz™**: crackle, cobblestone (available by the sheet)
• **vellum Paper Pizazz™**: pastel tan (*12"x12" Pastel Vellum Papers,* also by the sheet), metallic silver (*Metallic Silver,* also by the sheet)
• **solid Paper Pizazz™**: brown, cream (*Solid Jewel Tones*)
• **gold swirl, clock**: S. Axelrod Company
• **tiny gold brads**: Magic Scraps
• **black pen**: Zig® Writer
• **adhesive dots**: Glue Dots™
• **designer**: Toddi Barclay

#3 Horses and leather always go together! Paris used a brown leather paper for the background and overlayed a 6"x12" piece of torn vellum. She secured it to the left of the background with a snap in each corner. For the large center mat, Paris cut a 9½" square of brown embossed leather and matted it on gold. She matted each photo on torn vellum. To emphasize the large photo with color block matting, she cut a 5¾"x7½" piece of blue embossed leather and matted it on gold. Paris then matted a 2⅛"x7½" piece of brown embossed and centered it on the blue. She fashioned a lasso from twine and placed it under the photo. For the tag she cut 2¼" squares of blue embossed, gold and brown embossed and tore the top of each. She layered them on the tag as shown and trimmed the excess. Paris tied a piece of twine and Twistel™ to the tag. She journaled on vellum and tore the edges.

• **patterned Paper Pizazz™**: brown embossed leather, brown leather, blue floral embossed leather (*"Leather" Papers*)
• **specialty Paper Pizazz™**: metallic gold (*Metallic Gold,* also by the sheet), pastel tan vellum (*12"x12" Pastel Vellum Papers,* also by the sheet)
• **manilla tag**: Paper Reflections®
• **jute twine**: Darice, Inc.
• **gold snap, dusty blue Twistel™**: Making Memories™
• **black pen**: Zig® Writer
• **adhesive glue dots**: Glue Dots™
• **adhesive foam tape**: Therm O Web
• **designer**: Paris Dukes

#1 Pretty pink papers piled on the page! Lisa chose to emphasize the candid photo while still including the portrait.

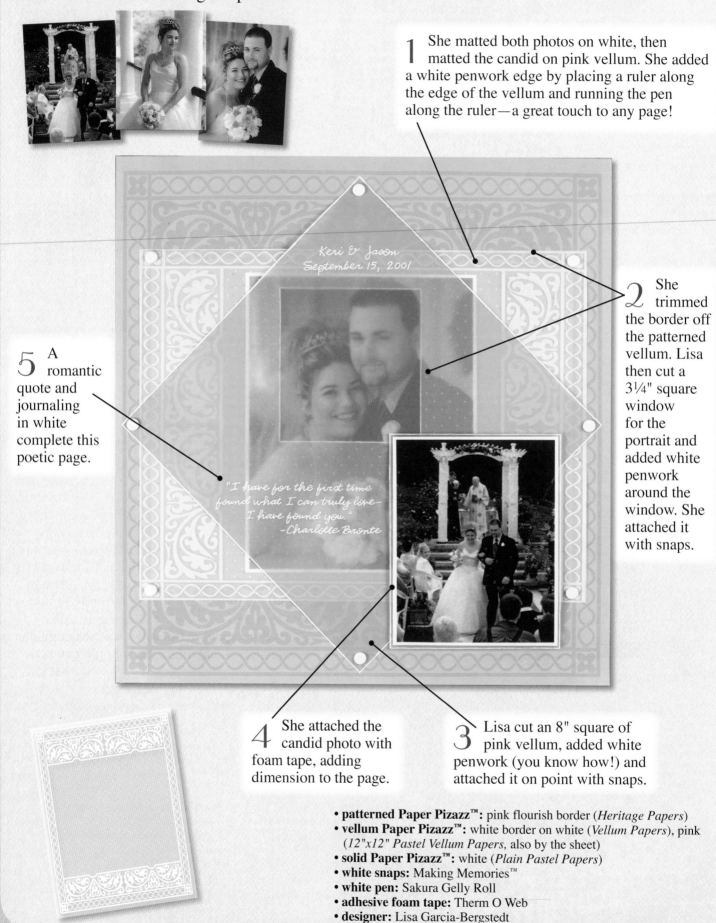

1 She matted both photos on white, then matted the candid on pink vellum. She added a white penwork edge by placing a ruler along the edge of the vellum and running the pen along the ruler—a great touch to any page!

Keri & Jason
September 15, 2001

"I have for the first time found what I can truly love—I have found you."
-Charlotte Bronte

2 She trimmed the border off the patterned vellum. Lisa then cut a 3¼" square window for the portrait and added white penwork around the window. She attached it with snaps.

5 A romantic quote and journaling in white complete this poetic page.

4 She attached the candid photo with foam tape, adding dimension to the page.

3 Lisa cut an 8" square of pink vellum, added white penwork (you know how!) and attached it on point with snaps.

- **patterned Paper Pizazz™:** pink flourish border (*Heritage Papers*)
- **vellum Paper Pizazz™:** white border on white (*Vellum Papers*), pink (*12"x12" Pastel Vellum Papers,* also by the sheet)
- **solid Paper Pizazz™:** white (*Plain Pastel Papers*)
- **white snaps:** Making Memories™
- **white pen:** Sakura Gelly Roll
- **adhesive foam tape:** Therm O Web
- **designer:** Lisa Garcia-Bergstedt

#2 Ribbons and roses combine to make this refreshing page! Paris matted each photo on mauve. She matted the large photo on plaid, then matted all the photos on vellum with room for beads. For the tag she cut a 3⅛"x2¼" piece of vellum, a 3⅛"x4½" piece of plaid and a 3⅛"x5¼" piece of mauve. She tore one short edge of each and layered them on the tag. Paris cut the wire in to three 3" lengths. She threaded five beads on two lengths and seven on the remaining length. She attached them to the page, bending the ends at the back and taping them to secure. She threaded the fibers through the tag and journaled on the plaid with the black pen. Paris cut a 3⅞"x11⅞" piece of vellum and attached it on the right side of the page. She overlayed a 13" length of ribbon and the tag.

- **patterned Paper Pizazz™:** rose/butterflies, green/mauve plaid (*Joy's Vintage Papers*)
- **vellum Paper Pizazz™:** sage green (*12"x12" Pastel Vellum Papers*)
- **solid Paper Pizazz™:** mauve (*Solid Muted Colors*)
- **multi-colored facted beads:** Blue Moon Beads/Elizabeth Ward & Co., Inc.
- **1½" wide moss green satin ribbon:** C.M. Offray & Son, Inc.
- **large white tag:** Paper Reflections® DMD Industries
- **fibers:** Adornaments™
- **24-gauge silver wire:** Colour Craft™
- **black pen:** Zebra Jimnie Gel Rollerball
- **glue dots:** Glue Dots™
- **designer:** Paris Dukes

#3 Layers of love–and vellum–add up to this romantic page. Arlene matted the large photo on gold then on a 6½"x8¼" piece of white vellum with gold penwork and chalked edges. For the wrapped frame she cut a 6½"x7¾" piece of peach vellum and tore the edges. She placed the vellum over the photo and tore a 1" wide frame. Arlene wrapped floss around the frame and tied a bow at the bottom. She cut a 4"x12" strip of white vellum, added gold penwork and chalked the edges. She cut a 3½"x12" strip of peach vellum and tore the edges. She matted the small photos on gold, placed them between the peach and white vellum and tore the windows. She computer journaled on white vellum, added gold penwork and chalked the edges. For the title she computer journaled on white vellum with a peach overlay. The gold charm ties together the gold elements on this peachy page.

- **patterned Paper Pizazz™:** floral, leaf (*Pretty Collage Papers*)
- **specialty Paper Pizazz™:** peach vellum, white vellum (*Vellum Papers,* also by the sheet), metallic gold (*Metallic Gold,* also by the sheet)
- **yellow-orange decorating chalk:** Craf-T Products
- **gold heart charm:** S. Axelrod Company
- **metallic gold embroidery floss:** DMC
- **gold pen:** Pentel of America Ltd.
- **designer:** Arlene Peterson

#1 Shauna hunted for just the right elements for this Easter page!

1 On the plaid background she attached a 10¾" ivory vellum square with an eyelet in each corner to ghost the paper.

2 She copied the photo from color to black and white so she could color select parts with the photo tinting pens. Then she matted it in the center of the sponged paper and chalked the edges.

7 She finished the page by tying a shoestring bow with the ribbon, attaching the letter charm to the circle tag with an eyelet and mounting it behind the bow with a glue dot.

3 She used the remainder of the sponged paper to cut a 9¼" square frame 1¼" wide and shaded it with chalks.

6 Shauna journaled with the black pen then attached the photo at an angle with foam tape.

5 To make the Easter grass she untwisted the Twistel™, cut 3" strips and glued them to the back of the frame. She used foam tape to attach the frame centered on the page.

4 With the leftover sponged paper she cut ¼" wide strips and chalked the edges. She glued them over the frame at an angle and wrapped any excess to the back.

- **patterned Paper Pizazz™:** yellow/blue/green plaid, gold sponged (*Mixing Light Papers*)
- **vellum Paper Pizazz™:** ivory (available by the sheet)
- **⅛" silver eyelets:** Stamp Studio
- **tan, light brown, dark brown, black decorating chalks:** Craf-T Products
- **18" of ⅞" wide sage green satin ribbon:** C.M. Offray & Son, Inc.
- **sage green Twistel™:** Making Memories®
- **circle tag:** Making Memories® Details™ Tagged™
- **Elegant Script eyelet letters:** Making Memories® Details™
- **photo tinting pens (foliage, lavender, blush, woodland, denim, honeycomb):** Zig® Photo Twins™
- **black pen:** Sakura Gelly Roll
- **adhesive foam tape:** Therm O Web
- **glue dots:** Glue Dots™
- **designer:** Shauna Berglund-Immel

#2 Griffin's sweater and jeans inspired this whimsical page. Lisa cropped each photo to 3¾"x4" then matted them on a single 12"x4½" strip of dark green paper. She cut a 12"x4" strip of white vellum and used the template to cut windows where she wanted to highlight part of the photo (see the Peek-a-boo windows, page 104). Lisa attached the vellum and the photos to the page center with an eyelet in each corner. She used the patterns on page 144 to cut out the eggs, grass, head, pants, shoes and hands. Journaling finished this delightful page.

- **patterned Paper Pizazz™:** yellow/green plaid (*Coordinating Florals & Patterns*), denim (available by the sheet)
- **solid Paper Pizazz™:** white, tan (*Plain Pastels,* also by the sheet), pale green, yellow, mauve (*Solid Muted Colors*), dark green, brown (*Solid Jewel Tones*)
- **⅛" dark green eyelets:** Stamp Studio
- **template:** *Paper Flair™ Windows #1 Template*
- **½" circle punch:** Marvy® Uchida
- **pink decorating chalk:** Craf-T Products
- **foam adhesive tape:** Therm O Web
- **black pens:** Sakura Micron, Sakura Opaque
- **designer:** Lisa Garcia-Bergstedt

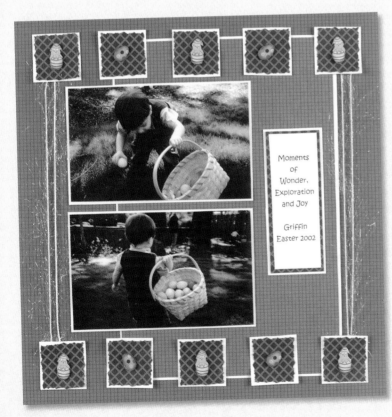

#3 Arlene created this treasure of a page with top and bottom borders that add pop and color. She cut the blue grid paper to 7"x10½", matted it on white and glued it off-center on the green grid background. She cut ten 1½" squares of green diamond paper and trimmed the edges with deckle scissors. She matted each one on white. Arlene cut individual eggs from easter egg paper and attached one to each square with foam tape. She glued the squares to the page with the fibers on either side. She matted the photos on white and glued them to the left side of the page, overlapping the grid papers. Arlene computer journaled on white and matted it on green diamond then white. Wonderful!

- **patterned Paper Pizazz™:** green grid, green diamond, blue grid (*12"x12" Bright Tints*), easter eggs (available by the sheet)
- **solid Paper Pizazz™:** white (*Plain Pastels*)
- **deckle decorative scissors:** Family Treasures, Inc.
- **white fibers:** Adornaments™
- **adhesive foam tape:** Therm O Web
- **designer:** Arlene Peterson

#1 Shauna made waves with this dynamic page!

1 She layered vellum papers over the sandstone background sheet then tore the top of each to reveal the color beneath. From the top of the page the vellums are: aqua, teal, sky blue, blue/lavender and white

2 She punched a square out of the bottom vellum strip and traced the edges with the silver pen.

3 She trimmed the vellum and sandstone papers to 11¾" then attached them to a 12"x12" piece of silver paper with an eyelet in each corner.

6 She stitched the beaded words to the tags and journaled with the black pen.

5 For the beaded photo corners Shauna inserted the needle from the back of the page, strung beads, crossed the photo corner and inserted the needle into the page.

4 She matted the photos on silver then used the photo tinting pens to highlight portions. She slid them into the vellum pockets then glued them to the page.

- **patterned Paper Pizazz™:** 12"x12" sandstone (available by the sheet)
- **specialty Paper Pizazz™:** white vellum (*Vellum Papers,* also by the sheet), aqua, teal, sky blue, blue/lavender pastel vellums (*Pastel Vellum Papers*), metallic silver (*Metallic Silver,* also available by the sheet)
- **1¾" square punch:** Marvy® Uchida
- **⅛" silver eyelets:** Stamp Studio

- **seed beads, beaded wire words:** Making Memories® Details™
- **rectangle, circle vellum tags:** Making Memories® Details™ Tagged™
- **silver thread:** DMC
- **photo tinting pens (blue jeans, honeycomb, peach glow, golden locks):** Zig® Photo Twins™
- **black, silver pen:** Sakura Gelly Roll
- **designer:** Shauna Berglund-Immel

#2 This page is just beachy! Arlene used creative matting to set off the family photo and the letters. She cut the center from the photo, matted it on blue paper and tan vellum with a torn edge. She matted the outer portion to match and aligned them on top of each other. Very clever, Arlene! The smaller photos were matted on torn tan vellum. For the letters she cut two sets from vellum, tore the tan letters and glued them to the blue. She computer journaled on tan vellum, tore the edges and matted it on torn blue vellum. The fiber across the bottom of the page added shine and texture.

- **patterned Paper Pizazz™:** beach collage (*Vacation Collage Papers*)
- **vellum Paper Pizazz™:** blue, tan (*Pastel Velum Paperse*, also by the sheet)
- **solid Paper Pizazz™:** blue (*Solid Muted Colors*)
- **school house letter die-cuts:** Accu-Cut®
- **fiber:** Adornaments™
- **designer:** Arlene Peterson

#3 Lisa swam to success with this pretty two-page spread. She started with two 8½"x11" white papers. She cut two 8½"x4" pieces of speckle paper, tore the top edge and glued them to the bottom of each page. She cut a 5¼"x11" piece of white paper with a 5¼"x8" piece of baby blue vellum glued to the top. She cut 5¼"x2" pieces of tan, ivory and cornflower blue vellum, tore the long edges and chalked each torn edge. She layered them and left white showing at the bottom. She cut the strip in half and glued one to the outside of each page. She cropped the small photos and stitched twine around them. Lisa computer journaled in a large font size on ivory vellum and tucked them behind the speckle paper, then matted the photos on black. She added finishing touches with twine borders, letters and journaling with the black pen.

- **patterned Paper Pizazz™:** speckle brown (*Soft & Subtle Textures*)
- **vellum Paper Pizazz™:** ivory (available by the sheet), baby blue, cornflower blue (*Pastel Vellum Papers*), tan (*Pastel Vellum Papers*, also by the sheet, white (*Vellum Papers*, also by the sheet)
- **solid Paper Pizazz™:** white (*Plain Pastel Papers*), black (*Solid Jewel Tones*)
- **brown, blue decorating chalks:** Craf-T Products
- **needle, brown thread**
- **hemp twine**
- **glue dots:** Glue Dots™
- **black pen:** Sakura Micron
- **designer:** Lisa Garcia-Bergstedt

#1 Shauna added interest, dimension and texture to this page when she used beads, buttons, fibers and eyelets–oh my! She used only the first three companion papers for this stunning page.

1 Shauna punched six flowers from the sponged paper, then used the rest as the background sheet.

2 She trimmed the posies paper to 8" wide, matted it on black then white trimmed with scallop scissors.

6 Shauna used three types of journaling—hand lettering, computer and alphabet beads. Eyelets emphasize and punctuate the page.

3 She matted the photo on black and scalloped white, then on a wider stripe paper. She went further and matted the stripes paper on black then white.

WALK WITH ME DADDY

the best is yet to be...

5 She embellished the photo with flowers on the bottom and a bow at the top.

4 She matted the punched flowers on black and stitched on the buttons. Then she attached them with Glue Dots™.

- **patterned Paper Pizazz**™: three burgundy & teal companion papers (*Mixing Bright Papers*)
- **solid Paper Pizazz**™: black (*Solid Jewel Tones*), white (*Plain Pastels*)
- **white, black eyelets:** Stamp Studio
- **black buttons:** Making Memories™
- **alphabet beads:** Darice®
- **sheer black ribbon:** C.M. Offray & Son, Inc.
- **white, black fibers:** DMC
- **flower punch:** Family Treasures, Inc.
- **scallop decorative scissors:** Fiskars®
- **black pen:** Sakura Gelly Roll
- **glue dots:** Glue Dots™
- **designer:** Shauna Berglund-Immel

#2 Brynnen lights up this page when combined with fun, bright patterns. Lisa matted the photos on black. She cut a 5⅞"x3" piece of diamonds and of white vellum. She matted the inside edges of the diamonds on black, journaled on the vellum and attached them to the page with eyelets. She colored the "B" with the burgundy brush pen. She cut a 5½"x8⅜" piece of stripe paper and matted the inside edges on black. She centered the large photo on top. Lisa cut a 5⅛"x11¼" piece of posies paper and matted the inside edges on black. She computer journaled on white vellum then cut it to 4⅞"x11¼", tore the bottom edge and chalked it. She cut the window and added black penwork. She glued the photo to the posies paper and overlayed the vellum, then attached them to the page with two eyelets at the top. She painted the button with the teal pen and added the wire accents. The mother charm added a touch of shine and dimension to the page.

- **patterned Paper Pizazz™:** four burgundy & teal companion papers (*Mixing Bright Papers*)
- **vellum Paper Pizazz™:** white (*Vellum Papers,* also by the sheet)
- **solid Paper Pizazz™:** black (*Solid Jewel Tones*)
- **black eyelets:** Stamp Studio
- **black wire:** Artistic Wire
- **heart button:** Making Memories™
- **"mother" eyelet charm:** Making Memories™
- **black, pink decorating chalk:** Craf-T Products
- **black, teal Painty, burgundy brush pens:** Zig®
- **designer:** Lisa Garcia-Bergstedt

#3 Arlene showcased two sisters on this exciting page! She tore two 2" wide strips of posies paper and attached one to the top and one to the bottom of the sponged background paper. For the page title she cut the letters from diamond paper then matted them on white and trimmed them with the deckle scissors. She matted "SISTERS" on stripe paper and again on white. Arlene created her own flower pattern, cut three from diamond paper and matted them on white. Arlene triple-matted the photo on white, stripe and white again. She computer journaled on white paper then cut them out with random angles. She cut a ⅝"x6¾" piece of stripe paper and matted it on white, then place the journaling on top. She used the white snaps and black floss to attach different elements to the page, adding dimension and texture.

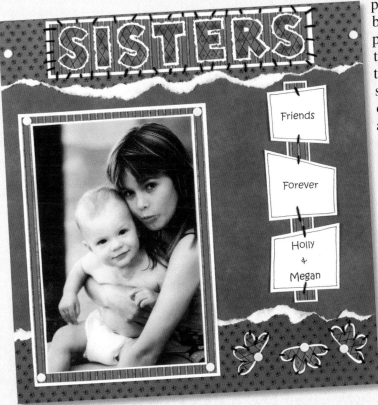

- **patterned Paper Pizazz™:** four burgundy & teal companion papers (*Mixing Bright Papers*)
- **solid Paper Pizazz™:** white (*Plain Pastels*)
- **white snaps:** Making Memories™
- **letter template:** EK Tracers Block
- **black embroidery floss:** DMC
- **deckle decorative scissors:** Fiskars®
- **black pen:** Sakura Gelly Roll
- **designer:** Arlene Peterson

#1 Lisa demonstrates simple elegance with this pretty and romantic page!

1 She triple-matted the photo on burgundy, navy blue and gold.

2 She cut an 8" square of white vellum and added gold penwork to the edges by placing a ruler along the edge of the vellum and running her gold pen along the ruler.

Peter & Joan
25 years

A successful
marriage requires
falling in love many times,
always with the same person.
—Mignon McLaughlin

3 She tore a 4½" wide strip off one of the collage papers and layered it over the white vellum. Then she added the matted photo on point in the center—what a neat look!

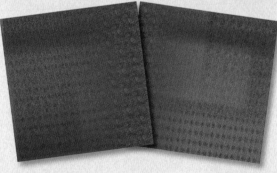

5 The page was set off by the gold journaling to match the gold matting paper.

4 She cut irises from the vellum paper and layered them over the photo.

- **patterned Paper Pizazz™:** two burgundy collage companion papers (*Pretty Collage Papers*)
- **specialty Paper Pizazz™:** white vellum (*Vellum Papers,* also by the sheet), iris velum (*Floral Vellum Papers*), metallic gold (*Metallic Gold,* also by the sheet)
- **solid Paper Pizazz™:** burgundy, navy blue (*Solid Jewel Tones*)
- **gold pen:** Sakura Gelly Roll
- **designer:** Lisa Garcia-Bergstedt

#2 Susan creates texture and depth with this layered motif. She stacked an 8" square of dark pink vellum, an 8½"x6¼" rectangle of white vellum and a 6" square of pink vellum in the center of the background page. She double-matted the photo on pink vellum then on silver. She used the template to cut shapes 1-B and 3-D from silver paper, 1-A from pink vellum and 3-C from dark pink vellum. She used the punches to embellish the shapes then layered them with foam tape. For the pink vellum box pleat she cut two 12"x1½" strips. She marked the strips in alternating incremetns of 1" and ½". Susan simply folded the vellum at each increment to form pin tuck pleats (see page 78). She punched a diamond in the center of each 1" pleat then she wove a ⅛" wide strip of silver paper throught the holes. Susan added silver penwork and journaling to set off the silver paper and add sparkle to the page.

- **patterned Paper Pizazz™:** burgundy collage (*Pretty Collage Papers*)
- **specialty Paper Pizazz™:** dark pink vellum pink vellum (*12"x12" Pastel Vellum Papers*), white vellum (*Vellum Papers,* also by the sheet), metallic silver (*Metallic Silver,* also by the sheet)
- **Paper Flair™ Nested Shapes template**

- **corner punches:** Marvy® Uchida, Family Treasures™
- **diamond punch:** Fiskars®
- **foam adhesive tape:** Therm O Web
- **silver pen:** Sakura Gelly Roll
- **designer:** Susan Cobb

#3 Arlene used big triangles to create sweet symmetry on this page! To make the vellum triangle she started with a 12"x12" piece and marked the center of one edge. She drew a line from the center point to each opposite corner and cut along the edges. She cut two 1½" wide vellum strips and placed them opposite the big triangle as shown. She cut two ½" wide gold strips and centered them on the vellum strips. Arlene wrapped two 13" lengths of floss around the left edge of the page. She cut out the two tags then cut a slit on the right side of the tassel and slid the small tag inside. She matted both tags on gold and placed them on the floss. Arlene matted the photo on gold and centered it on the page. She added the finishing touch with gold journaling and penwork.

- **patterned Paper Pizazz™:** burgundy collage (*Pretty Collage Papers*)
- **specialty Paper Pizazz™:** pastel tan vellum (*12"x12" Pastel Vellum Papers,* also by the sheet), metallic gold (*Metallic Gold,* also by the sheet)
- **Paper Pizazz™ Cut-outs™:** burgundy & lace tags (*Tag Art*)
- **gold embroidery floss:** DMC
- **gold pen:** Pentel of America, Ltd.
- **designer:** Arlene Peterson

#1 Tags, stamps and letters bring this rugged page to life!

1 Shauna trimmed the fatigue paper to 10" square and matted it on gold, then tan vellum.

2 She matted the photo on five papers—gold, vellum, paisley, copper and vellum!

3 She inserted an eyelet in each corner of the page and strung a gold thread border.

4 She cut "Good Old Boys" from *Alphabet Tiles,* then matted "Old" on gold paper and overlayed vellum with eyelets. She attached "Good" and "Boys" to the page with varying layers of foam tape for depth.

8 Lastly, she carefully tore out the stamps and mounted them with varying layers of foam tape.

5 Shauna cut out the tags, matted them on copper paper and attached them together with an eyelet and fibers.

7 Shauna chalked the torn vellum for a distressed, worn look. Then she outlined the vellum mats with the copper pen.

6 She computer journaled on vellum then attached it to the tag with three randomly placed eyelets

- **patterned Paper Pizazz™:** green paisley, green fatigue, green texture (*Mixing Masculine Papers*)
- **specialty Paper Pizazz™:** copper (*Heavy Metal*), gold (*Metallic Gold,* also by the sheet), tan vellum (*Pastel Vellum Papers,* also by the sheet)
- **Paper Pizazz™ Cut-outs™:** heritage tags & stamps (*Tag Art Cut-outs*), letters (*Alphabet Tiles*)
- **brown, black decorating chalks:** Craf-T Products
- **gold thread:** DMC
- **⅛", ³⁄₁₆" copper eyelets:** Stamp Studio
- **foam adhesive tape:** Therm O Web
- **copper pen:** Jimnie Gel Rollerball
- **fibers:** Adornments
- **designer:** Shauna Berglund-Immel

#2 All hands on board! Lisa created this strong yet subtle page using companion papers with the paisley as a background. She matted an 8" square of green textured paper and a 7½" square of fatigue paper on black then attached them offset with eyelets. She used copper thread to add a touch of sparkle to the page. Lisa matted the photo on sage green, olive green and black. She punched the hands from copper foil and inserted an eyelet in each. She attached them as photo corners to the page with more copper thread. Simple copper journaling adds punch to the page. The punched hands mirror the boys and the copper shines all over this page.

- **patterned Paper Pizazz™:** green paisley, green fatigue, green texture (*Mixing Masculine Papers*)
- **solid Paper Pizazz™:** black, light sage green, olive green (*Solid Jewel Tones*)
- **copper eyelets:** Stamp Studio
- **copper thread:** DMC
- **hand print punch:** McGill, Inc.
- **copper foil:** American Art Clay Co.
- **copper pen:** Sakura Gelly Roll
- **designer:** Lisa Garcia-Bergstedt

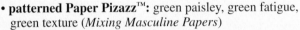

#3 Arlene made this page striking by adding dimensional touches like buttons and string. She matted a 7⅝"x10¾" piece of dimonds paper on black. She matted an 11"x1¼" piece of rose paper on black, then placed a 12"x1" piece of green fatigue on top. She added jute borders on the top and bottom and glued fish buttons between the jute. Arlene quadruple-matted the photo on rose, black, paisley and black again. She wrapped jute around the corners and added more fish buttons. She computer journaled on green fatigue then double matted on rose and black. More jute and buttons continue the theme. What a great way to capture the memories of a fun day in Seattle, Washington!

- **patterned Paper Pizazz™:** green paisley, green fatigue, green texture, green/rose diamonds (*Mixing Masculine Papers*)
- **solid Paper Pizazz™:** black (*Solid Jewel Tones*), rose (*Solid Muted Tints*)
- **jute string:** Westrim® Crafts
- **fish buttons:** Dress It Up
- **designer:** Arlene Peterson

WHILE YOU WERE OUT

5/4/02   Hour 3:15

M Diana Robinson

Of

Phone Area Code 916 Phone # 233-7348

FAX Area Code	Phone #	
Telephoned	Returned Call	Left Package
Please Call	Was In	Please See Me
Will Call Again	Will Return	Important

Message Looking for ways to make her own tag art. Can we help?

PARAMOUNT GRAPHICS INC.
"Advancing the state of your art."

India Harbert
5698 Hobbs St.
West limestone, CA 90210

37 USA

Bev & Bob Nunn
4685 Muthers RD.
Edenburn PA. 16816

WHILE YOU WERE OUT

Date 8/10/02   Hour 3:15

To

M Karen Fairbanks

Of

Phone Area Code 806 Phone # 299-0472

FAX Area Code	Phone #	
Telephoned	✓ Returned Call	Left Package
Please Call	Was In	Please See Me
Will Call Again	Will Return	Important ✓

Message Stickers are taking over her cropping room. She needs layout ideas for stickers-situation is getting desperate!

Signed KS

©AVERY REORDER NO. 47296   Made With

RUSH
1.

from: scrappinaddict@usa.com

scrappinquestins@hotp.com

Date: Monday, November 25, 2002

Subject: Boy Pages

I have three sons, four nephews, two bro...
father. I love flowered paper and pretty...
with eleven guys to scrapbook. I NEED...
help?

Signed,

Scrappin' With The Guys

Dear Paper Pizazz,
I love the look of tag art on scrapbook pages and I want to start making my own tags. Do you have any ideas or tips for tags?
Sincerely,
Amy Nelson

Dear Customer Service
...scrapbook

CANADA 65

Teddy

Paper Pizazz
1250 N.W. third
Dept C-12 PK2
Canby, OR
97013

97013+3440

You Asked For It!

You wrote. You called. You e-mailed. You asked for, pleaded—and in some cases, demanded—more ideas about four very specific scrapbooking topics. Masculine themes, tag art, stickers and vellum topped the list of our most frequently asked questions.

First—masculine themes. From mothers of sons to those who want to scrapbook photos of brothers, nephews, husbands and boyfriends, we heard you. It seems that the guys in our lives can be really tough—to scrapbook. And while you can change the layouts throughout this book from feminine to masculine, we know it helps to have designer pages to get you started.

Tag art has taken the scrapbooking world by storm. Suddenly, the humble tag has graduated to stylish scrapbook embellishment. Wondering how to create your own designer tags? Let us show you how to turn the tag into a clever, personalized page accent.

Stickers, a scrapbooking staple, can also pose a creative challenge. They're so easy to buy! They're so easy, in fact, that you might have a stash of unused stickers. The Scrapbook Specialists have terrific ideas for turning that sticker stash into wonderful, whimsical page embellishments. (Disclaimer: This does mean, of course, that you may buy more stickers.)

"What can I do with vellum?" This has been THE question for scrapbookers for the past few years. Now, as scrappers have mastered matting and punching with vellum, the overwhelming question is: "What ELSE can I do with vellum?" We have the answers. Just turn the page!

B oys, boys, boys! This strong page is fun and masculine at the same time.

1 A brown-tone plaid was cut to 7¼"x9½" and centered on the page.

2 Vellum isn't just for pretty pages. Lisa wrinkled up a torn 9"x11" piece for this rough and tumble boy page. After flattening it she tore small holes and chalked the edges.

3 She stitched the vellum to the page with gold thread, making simple "X's."

7 The black pen was perfect for journaling both in cursive and in print.

4 Lisa cut a 12"x3¼" vellum strip then used a ruler and the gold pen to highlight the edges. The ¼" brads were used to attach it to the page.

6 By matting the photo on gold paper Lisa picks up the gold in the background collage paper, the gold brads and the gold penwork on the vellum.

5 The tag art letters were cut out and attached with ³⁄₁₆" brads. Notice how she mixed the brad sizes.

- **patterned Paper Pizazz™:** brown collage (*Masculine Collage Papers*), brown plaid (by the sheet), letter tags (*Tag Art*, also by the sheet)
- **specialty Paper Pizazz™:** ivory vellum (*Pastel Vellum Papers,* also by the sheet), gold metallic (*Metallic Gold,* also by the sheet)

- **brown decorating chalks:** Craf-T Products
- **⅛", ¼" gold brads:** HyGlo/American Pin
- **gold thread, needle**
- **black pen:** Sakura Micron
- **gold pen:** Sakura Gelly Roll
- **designer:** Lisa Garcia-Bergstedt

Dreams can come true… as Arlene illustrates in this page. She cut off the right border of one background paper, then she used an X-acto® knife to cut along the ends of the anchors. She put a brad in the center of the compass and wheel then attached a ¼"x12" silver strip to the back of the left edge of the anchor strip. Arlene added dimension to the page by putting foam tape under the end of each anchor. A 3"x12" piece of vellum was then attached to the back of the anchors and silver so ¾" of the vellum is on the left side. She then attached the strips to the background paper, making sure the page was 12" wide. Arlene tied five knots similar to those on the background paper, then attached them to the vellum. She cut a 4¾"x7" piece of vellum then attached a 2⅜"x7" piece of tan paper even with the left edge of the vellum with brads. She matted the photo on silver. A ½"x6¼" piece of tan was then was attached to the right back of the matted photo. Arlene computer journaled on vellum, matted it on silver, then added tan vellum and solid as above but reversing the side.

- **patterned Paper Pizazz™:** 2 nautical companion papers (*Masculine Collage Papers*)
- **specialty Paper Pizazz™:** silver (*Metallic Silver,* also by the sheet), tan vellum (*Pastel Vellum Papers,* also by the sheet)
- **solid Paper Pizazz™:** tan (*Solid Jewel Tones*)
- **³⁄₁₆" gold brads:** HyGlo/American Pin
- **X-acto® knife:** Hunt Mfg.
- **jute string:** Westrim Crafts
- **adhesive foam tape:** Therm O Web
- **designer:** Arlene Peterson

The great outdoors are brought inside on this dynamic page. Arlene likes to use collage papers to highlight special photos for a quick and stunning page. First, she cut a 8½"x6½" piece of gold paper and glued it centered on the page. Then she cut a 8½"x10" piece of vellum and tore the upper-left and bottom-right corners at an angle. She highlighted the straight vellum edges with the gold pen. Arlene matted the photo on gold then on forest green paper. The brads add dimension and a punch of gold. By journaling with a computer on vellum, then highlighting the edges with the gold pen the text is subtle, yet effective, letting the picture be the centerpiece of the page.

- **patterned Paper Pizazz™:** green leaf, mountain collage (*Vacation Collage Papers*)
- **specialty Paper Pizazz™:** gold (*Metallic Gold,* also by the sheet), green vellum (*Pastel Vellum Papers,* also by the sheet)
- **solid Paper Pizazz™:** forest green (*Solid Jewel Tones*)
- **¼" gold brads:** HyGlo/American Pin
- **adhesive foam tape:** Therm O Web
- **gold, black pen:** Sakura Micron
- **designer:** Arlene Peterson

Travelling to foreign places can create wonderful memories. This page put those treasures on paper. Lisa double-matted each photo first on black and on copper-brown. Then she journaled on a 3"x12" piece of vellum, tore and chalked the left edge and attached it flush with the right edge of the page. Lisa tore a 2" square window 2" from the top of the vellum. Then the tore a stamp from the companion page, chalked the edges and attached it in the window with foam tape. By tearing out pieces from the companion page to place by the photos, Lisa compliments the old photos and ties the whole page together. Journaling and photo captions complete the story.

- **patterned Paper Pizazz™:** 2 travel companion papers (*Masculine Collage Papers*)
- **vellum Paper Pizazz™:** tan (*Pastel Vellum Papers,* also by the sheet)
- **solid Paper Pizazz™:** black, copper-brown (*Solid Jewel Tones*)
- **brown decorating chalk:** Craf-T Products
- **adhesive foam tape:** Therm O Web
- **black pen:** Sakura Micron
- **designer:** Lisa Garcia-Bergstedt

Dads and tools go hand-in-hand on this fabulous page! Lisa put the papers to work to showcase this Dad's craftmanship. First she cut a 4¼"x12" piece of vellum and tore both long edges. Then she matted the photo on gray-blue paper with a ¼" border and centered it between the vellum and the edge of the page. The tools were cut from the companion paper and attached to the vellum with foam tape. She added a gold brad for the "nail," red pen for the "paint," a silver brad for the "screw" and wood bits for the "shavings." For the level, she drew a white line then attached the level with foam tape. Simple journaling completes the page.

- **patterned Paper Pizazz™:** tools companion papers (*Masculine Collage Papers*)
- **vellum Paper Pizazz™:** white (*Vellum Papers,* also by the sheet)
- **solid Paper Pizazz™:** gray-blue (*Solid Jewel Tones*)
- **³⁄₁₆" gold, silver brads:** HyGlo/American Pin
- **adhesive foam tape:** Therm O Web
- **black, red, white pens:** Sakura Micron
- **designer:** Lisa Garcia-Bergstedt

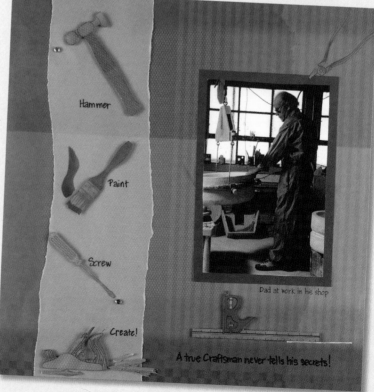

What a Ketchy page! Lisa made this page pop with black and white papers. She computer journaled the "ten things I love about Ketch" on a 4½"x10" piece of white vellum then attached it to the left side of black stripe paper with eyelets. She cut a 8"x12" piece of gray tiles paper and glued it to the right side of the stripe background. Lisa cut a 5¾" square of white tiles paper and matted it on black. She placed it on point on the gray paper. She computer journaled on a 7½" square of white vellum and attached it on top with eyelets. She matted the photo on black and placed it in the center. Lisa threaded black floss through the eyelets to create subtle texture and depth.

- **patterned Paper Pizazz™**: black, gray, white companion papers (*Mixing Masculine*)
- **vellum Paper Pizazz™**: white (*Vellum Papers*, also by the sheet)
- **solid Paper Pizazz™**: black (*Solid Jewel Tones*)
- ³⁄₁₆" **silver eyelets**: Stamp Studio
- **black embroidery floss**: DMC
- **silver pens**: Sakura Gelly Roll
- **designer**: Lisa Garcia-Bergstedt

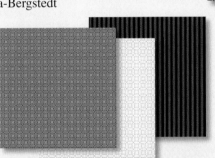

Lisa drafted up a wonderful masculine page for this dad! She used a collage background paper and added just a few elements. Lisa matted the photo on navy blue. She computer journaled on a 4½"x12" vellum and tore each long edge. Then she tore out a window to show the drafing elements on the background. She journal on a 5¼"x2¾" vellum and attached both journaling blocks with silver eyelets, bringing a flash of color to the page.

- **patterned Paper Pizazz™**: blue drafting collage (*Mixing Masculine*)
- **vellum Paper Pizazz™**: white (*Vellum Papers*, also by the sheet)
- **solid Paper Pizazz™**: navy blue (*Solid Jewel Tones*)
- ¼" **silver eyelets**: Stamp Studio
- **black pens**: Sakura Micron, Sakura Opaque
- **designer**: Lisa Garcia-Bergstedt

Romance, flowers and a happy couple make this page dazzle! Shauna captured the essence of this wedding day in this pretty-in-pink page.

1 For the main photo she triple-matted it on gold, diamonds collage and vellum. Outlining each mat with the gold pen makes the photo pop.

2 Shauna cut the bottom photos to the same size and matted each on gold. She placed vellum on top to ghost them. She journaled in black and attached them to the page with 1/8" eyelets continuing the gold accents.

6 One of the punched windows became an interesting element after Shauna glued on a flower, wrapped it in thread, journaled and attached it to the page with foam tape.

5 Shauna inserted a 1/8" eyelet in the top of each tag and outlined each with gold pen. She journaled, wrapped them with pearls, thread and charms. She attached them to the page with foam tape and topped each tag off with a bow.

4 She placed flowers between two layers of vellum then attached them to the back of each tag.

3 Shauna used the template to cut two tags from diamonds collage paper. Then she punched a window in each tag.

- **patterned Paper Pizazz™:** 2 pink diamonds collage companion papers (*Pretty Collage Papers,* also by the sheet)
- **specialty Paper Pizazz™:** pastel pink vellum (*Pastel Vellum Papers,* also by the sheet), gold (*Metallic Gold,* also by the sheet)
- **Paper Flair™ Tags template**
- **gold charms:** S. Axelrod Co.
- **3/16", 1/8" gold eyelets:** Stamp Studio
- **16" of 1/2" wide sheer burgundy ribbon:** C.M. Offray & Son, Inc.
- **pressed flowers**
- **1 3/4" square punch:** Marvy® Uchida
- **metallic gold thread**
- **adhesive foam tape:** Therm O Web
- **black, gold pens:** Sakura Micron, Gelly Roll
- **designer:** Shauna Berlund-Immel

Boys love to climb trees—and Arlene loves to make fabulous pages like this one! She used the pattern on page 142 to cut the tree branch from brown diamond paper and matted it on black. She punched the leaves from vellum and outlined the edges and drew in veins with the green pen. She cut out tags using the pattern below from green diamond paper. Arlene used a computer to journal the letters on vellum, and glued one on top of each tag. Matting each tag on black helps them pop off the background. Arlene added texture by carefully tearing all three layers of each tag, inserting eyelets and tying them to the branch with floss. She matted both the photos on black, brown swirl and on black again. For corners she cut 1" squares in half diagonally to make eight triangles, matted each on black and attached them to the photos with eyelets. Arlene journaled on vellum, matted on brown diamond and finally on black.

- **patterned Paper Pizazz™**: black with brown swirls, brown diamond, green grid, green mesh (*12"x12" Jewel Tints*)
- **vellum Paper Pizazz™**: green (*Pastel Vellum Papers,* also by the sheet)
- **solid Paper Pizazz™**: black (*Solid Jewel Tones*)
- **tree branch die-cuts:** Accu/Cut®
- **1" leaf punch:** Marvy® Uchida
- **brown eyelets:** Stamp Studio
- **copper embroidery floss:** DMC
- **adhesive foam tape:** Therm O Web
- **green pen:** Sakura Micron
- **designer:** Arlene Peterson

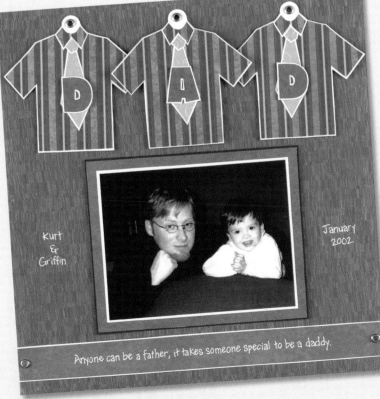

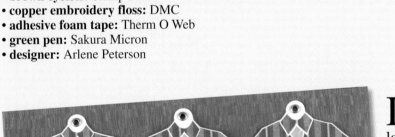

Dads are special, so Lisa created this fun page to celebrate them. She journaled on a 12"x1" lavender strip matted on white and attached it to the page with eyelets. Lisa matted the photo on white, then on lavender and on navy blue. She attached it to the page with foam tape for depth. Lisa used the patterns on page 141 to cut out the shirts and ties. She matted each piece on white with 1/32" borders, arranged them and attached to the page with foam tape, with the center shirt on top. After cutting the letters from lavender, she matted them on white with 1/32" borders and attached them with foam tape.

- **patterned Paper Pizazz™**: blue strokes, lavender stripes, lavender (*Mixing Heritage Papers*), yellow swirl (*Bright Tints,* also by the sheet)
- **solid Paper Pizazz™**: white (*Plain Pastel Papers*), navy blue (*Solid Jewel Tones*)
- **1/4" silver eyelets:** Stamp Studio
- **Fat Caps lettering template:** Francis Meyer
- **adhesive foam tape:** Therm O Web
- **white pen:** Sakura Gelly Roll
- **designer:** Lisa Garcia-Bergstedt

Stripes, dots and fun! Babies always bring a smile, just like this page Lisa created. For the background: She tore off 1½"-2" of the top edge of green stripes paper and put a 3" piece of blue textured behind it. She cut a 8"x4" piece of green dots and tore it in uneven halves and glued them to an 8"x5¾" piece of yellow plaid. Lisa then used the 4" and 2¾" circle patterns on page 144 to cut out the photos. She triple-matted each one on white, lime green and blue textured then she overlapped them with foam tape. Lisa used the letter templates and blue textured paper then double-matted them on white and lime green. To make the serendipity circles she cut a 12"x3" strip of blue textured paper and glued torn pices of the other papers to it. Then she cut four 2¼" circles using the pattern, inserted an eyelet in each and attached the letters with foam tape. Lisa tied floss to each eyelet and taped the floss to the back of the page. She finished off the page with simple journaling.

- **patterned Paper Pizazz™:** green stripes, blue textured, green dots, yellow plaid (*Mixing Baby Papers*)
- **solid Paper Pizazz™:** white (*Solid Pastel Papers*), lime green (*Soild Bright Papers*)
- **Fat Caps lettering template:** Francis Meyer
- **⅛" lime green eyelets:** Stamp Studio
- **lime green embroidery floss:** DMC
- **adhesive foam tape:** Therm O Web
- **black pen:** Sakura Micron
- **designer:** Lisa Garcia-Bergstedt

Babies live in onesies. Lisa turned a wardrobe classic into creative tags for this darling page. She matted the photo on white and on vellum, then she used brads and washers to attach it to the page. She used the pattern on page 141 to cut three onesies from white paper. Lisa cut out three animal tiles and stitched one to each onsie. Then she used the pattern above to make three wire hangers, taped one to the back of each, attached them to the page with foam tape and "hung" the hangers between the brads and washers. Along the bottom of the page Lisa cut a 10½"x1½" piece from animal tiles and matted it on white. She overlayed a 11⅛"x¾" piece of vellum and attached the group to the page with a brad in each end. Simple journaling completed the page.

- **patterned Paper Pizazz™:** stripes, animal tiles (*Mixing Baby Papers*)
- **vellum Paper Pizazz™:** blue (*Pastel Vellum Papers,* also by the sheet)
- **solid Paper Pizazz™:** white (*Solid Pastel Papers*)
- **blue thread, needle**
- **³⁄₁₆" gold brads, gold**
- **washers:** HyGlo/American Pin
- **16-gauge gold wire:** Artistic Wire Ltd.
- **adhesive foam tape:** Therm O Web
- **black pen:** Sakura Micron
- **designer:** Lisa Garcia-Bergstedt

A classic sport, fishing is Mike's favorite pastime. Lisa captured the spirit of the rod and reel in this simple, yet effective page. She used the patterns below to cut the fish from vellum, then outlined each with the copper pen. She inserted an eyelet into the "mouth" of each fish, then stitched each to the page with brown thread. She used the white pen to highlight the fishing line and to journal. For the small fish she punched out letters to spell "salmon." Lisa triple-matted the photo on terra cotta, on navy blue and finally on teal.

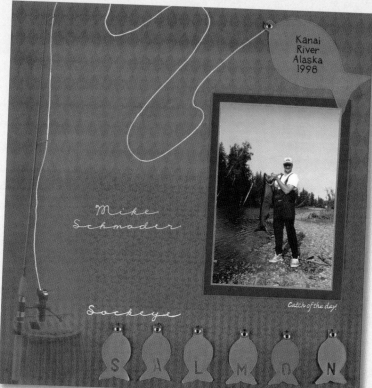

- **patterned Paper Pizazz™:** fishing pole (*Masculine Collage*)
- **vellum Paper Pizazz™:** peach (*Pastel Vellum Papers,* also by the sheet)
- **solid Paper Pizazz™:** terra cotta, navy blue, teal (*Solid Jewel Tones*)
- **⅛" copper eyelets:** Stamp Studio
- **letter punch:** Marvy® Uchida
- **brown thread, needle**
- **black pen:** Sakura Micron
- **white, copper pen:** Sakura Gelly Roll
- **designer:** Lisa Garcia-Bergstedt

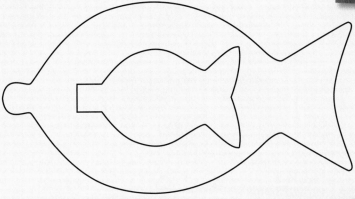

Rub-a-dub-dub there's a cute kid in the tub! This bubbly page dances with the addition of star-shaped tags. Lisa matted the photo and the computer journaling on blue paper. She cut the letters from blue swirl, matted them on white then inserted blue eyelets. Attaching them with foam tape allowed the floss to move on the page. She used the pattern above to cut four yellow vellum stars then inserted a yellow eyelet in each. After journaling with the black pen she tied the stars to the letters. Tags can be star shaped, too!

- **patterned Paper Pizazz™:** bubbles, blue swirls (both available by the sheet)
- **vellum Paper Pizazz™:** yellow (*Pastel Vellum Papers,* also by the sheet)
- **solid Paper Pizazz™:** white (*Plain Pastel Papers*), blue (*Solid Jewel Tones*)
- **marshmellow die-cut letters :** Accu/Cut®
- **⅛" blue, yellow eyelets:** Stamp Studio
- **yellow embroidery floss:** DMC
- **black pen:** Sakura Micron
- **adhesive foam tape:** Therm O Web
- **designer:** Lisa Garcia-Bergstedt

Crazy clowns just clownin' around! This festive page reflects birthday party fun. Shuana likes to use tags of different sizes, sometimes grouped together.

7 The large and medium tags were tied together with fiber then attached to the page with foam tape.

1 Shauna trimmed the blue checks paper to 10¾"x8¼", matted it on black and attached it to the swirl background.

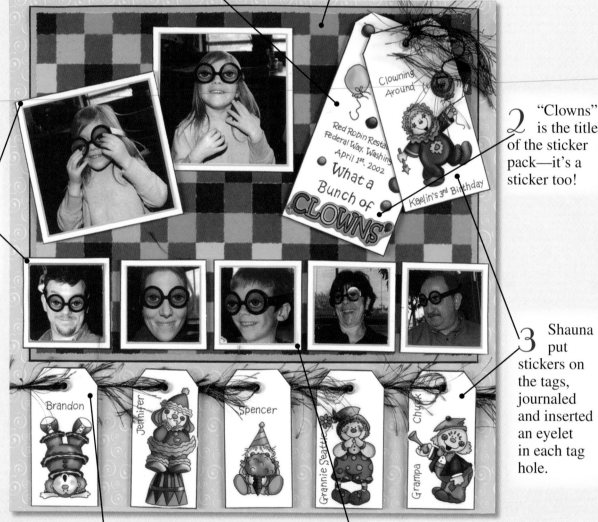

2 "Clowns" is the title of the sticker pack—it's a sticker too!

6 Shauna outlined the tags and photo mats with black pen to unify all the elements.

3 Shauna put stickers on the tags, journaled and inserted an eyelet in each tag hole.

5 The small tags were attached along the bottom of the page with foam tape for depth, then she threaded fiber through the tags and secured it to the back.

4 She used the square punch for the small photos, matted them on bright colors and then on white. The same matting was used for the large photos.

- **patterned Paper Pizazz™**: yellow swirl (*Bright Tints,* also by the sheet), blue checks (*A Girl's Scrapbook,* also by the sheet)
- **solid Paper Pizazz™**: yellow, pink, blue, lime green (*Bright Tints*), white (*Plain Pastels*), black (*Solid Jewel Tones*)
- **Paper Pizazz™ stickers**: *Annie Lang's Clowns*
- **Paper Flair™ Tags Template**

- **1¾" square punch**: Marvy® Uchida
- **¼" pink eyelets**: Stamp Studio
- **black fiber**: Adornaments™
- **black pen**: Sakura Micron
- **foam adhesive tape**
- **designer**: Shauna Berglund-Immel

There's nothing like the bond between children and their pets. Shauna customized this clever page to showcase each pet. She cut three 3" squares of vellum and stitched them evenly spaced ½" from the bottom of the barnwood background. She placed a sticker on each. Shauna used the pattern on page 142 to cut the bone tags, shaded them with the chalks and inserted a taupe eyelet into each. She punched the photos, matted them on brown, glued one to each tag and journaled. For the "leashes" Shauna cut three 7" lengths of Twistel™, looped one end and secured it with rusted wire. She tied the loose ends to the tags and slipped them into the pockets. The two large photos were first matted on brown then on ivory and the edges shaded with the chalks. The 11"x½" brown paper "collar" has eyelets and chalked edges. Shauna layered it over the photos. The heart was punched from metal and attached to the collar with wire circles. The paw print buttons finished the page.

- **patterned Paper Pizazz™**: barnwood (by the sheet)
- **velllum Paper Pizazz™**: ivory (by the sheet)
- **solid Paper Pizazz™**: ivory (*Plain Pastels*), brown (*Solid Muted Colors*)
- **Paper Pizazz™ stickers**: Annie Lang's Kids and Pets
- **brown, black decorating chalks**: Craf-T Products
- **1¾" square, ⅞" heart punches**: Marvy® Uchida
- **antique gold thread**: DMC
- **granite Twistel™**: Making Memories™
- **16-gauge silver, rusted wire**: Artistic Wire Ltd.
- **silver embossing metal**: Art Emboss™
- **³⁄₁₆" taupe, ⅛" silver eyelets**: Stamp Studio
- **paw print buttons**: Dress It Up
- **black pen**: Sakura Micron
- **photography**: I.N.V.U. Portraits by Helen
- **designer**: Shauna Berglund-Immel

This enchanting page came to life with the addition of stickers. Lisa cast her spell when she layered white vellum over lavender swirls for the background. She tore a 12"x4" piece of purple moiré for the bottom. Lisa triple-matted the photo on white, purple and white again. She matted the stickers on white paper. Eyelets were inserted in two then threaded with floss. By attaching the stickers with two layers of foam tape they seem to float on the page and the floss was secured to the back with clear tape. Journaled with fancy capital letters and a clever message, this royal page is complete!

- **patterned Paper Pizazz™**: purple moiré, lavender swirls (*Great Backgrounds*)
- **vellum Paper Pizazz™**: white (*Vellum Papers,* also by the sheet)
- **solid Paper Pizazz™**: purple (*Solid Jewel Tones*), white (*Plain Pastel Papers*)
- **Paper Pizazz™ stickers**: Annie Lang's Wizards and Dragons
- **white embroidery floss**: DMC
- **⅛" gold eyelets**: Stamp Studio
- **black pen**: Sakura Micron
- **adhesive foam tape**: Therm O Web

Fighting Dragons by day, chasing Wizards at night... the life of a Royal Knight is really tough!

Spooks on parade! This wacky page reflects the fun and playful spirit of Halloween. Shauna started by matting each photo on orange, then on black. She used the black pen to trace the template letters onto orange, shaded them with chalks and matted them on black. Shauna journaled the title and date, then added the cobwebs and penwork. The spider stickers run around the letters while the costumed kid stickers provide an easy, yet spirited border.

- **patterned Paper Pizazz™:** red sponged (*Mixing Bright Patterned Papers*)
- **solid Paper Pizazz™:** orange (*Solid Muted Colors*), black (*Solid Jewel Tones*)
- **Paper Pizazz™ stickers:** *Annie Lang's Halloween*
- **orange, yellow decorating chalks:** Craf-T Products
- **ABC tracers block letters:** EK Success Ltd.
- **black pen:** Sakura Micron
- **designer:** Shauna Berglund-Immel

Dynamite dinosaurs make this page roar! Arlene likes to line up photos and borders to create balance. She cut two pieces of green scuffed paper: 4½"x11" and 6"x11". She tore the edges, matted both on black and inserted an eyelet in each corner. For the photos she matted both the same: on black, blue brush strokes and again on black. To make sure the stickers didn't fade into the background Arlene put them on black then cut them out. She put the "Dinosaurs" sticker title on blue paper matted on black. Then it was put on a 3"x1" piece of blue brush strokes. For the remaining hanging sections she cut three 3"x2" pieces. All were matted on black. Arlene used computer journaling matted on black. The final embellishment was inserting the eyelets and stringing the sections together.

- **patterned Paper Pizazz™:** green scuffed/sponged, blue scuffed/sponged, blue brush strokes (*Great Jewel Backgrounds*)
- **solid Paper Pizazz™:** black, blue (*Solid Jewel Tones*), white (*Plain Pastels*)
- **Paper Pizazz™ stickers:** *Annie Lang's Dinosaurs*
- **blue embroidery floss:** DMC
- **⅛" black eyelets:** Stamp Studio
- **paw print buttons:** Dress It Up
- **designer:** Arlene Peterson

Our Little Angel! Shauna used penwork to unify all the elements on this charming page. She started with a 5⅜"x12" piece of white glued to the gingham background even with the right edge. She cut a 5¼"x3⅞" piece of each color of swirls. For cards she folded white paper in half and cut three 4"x3" pieces with the fold on the short edge. She glued each card on a swirls paper then embellished with stickers and journaling. Shauna computer journaled wishes for Bailey on white then matted each one on yellow. The photo and sticker blocks were matted on yellow then on white. Shauna added stickers and penwork before attaching them to the left side of the layout. A cheerful page with heartfelt journaling for baby Bailey!

- **patterned Paper Pizazz™**: blue swirls, yellow swirls, pink swirls, yellow gingham (*Bright Tints,* also by the sheet)
- **solid Paper Pizazz™**: yellow, pink, blue, lime green (*Bright Tints*), white (*Plain Pastels*), yellow (*Plain Brights*)
- **Paper Pizazz™ stickers**: *Annie Lang's Little Angels*
- **black pen**: Sakura Micron
- **yellow pen**: Zig® Writer
- **designer**: Shauna Berglund-Immel

inside the cards

Special friends deserve special pages. Shauna created a wall of framed photos for her "gallery" page. She matted six stickers on white paper with ¼" borders, then matted them on black with 1/16" borders. The photos were matted on black, white and black again. For picture hangers Shauna cut six 4½" lengths of wire, threaded one through each button and curled the ends. She attached one above each photo with glue dots. The title from the sticker pack is placed on a 3¾"x1¾ piece of white matted on black. Journaling completed this picture perfect page!

- **patterned Paper Pizazz™**: blue grid (*12"x12" Bright Tints*)
- **solid Paper Pizazz™**: white (*Plain Pastels*), black (*Solid Jewel Tones*)
- **Paper Pizazz™ stickers**: *Janie Dawson's Picture Perfect*
- **22-gauge black wire**: Artistic Wire Ltd.
- **blue buttons**: Dress It Up
- **black pen**: Sakura Micron
- **glue dots**: Glue Dots™
- **designer**: Shauna Berglund-Immel

Fit for a princess, this star-studded page combines vellum and metallic papers with glittering success. Shauna started with a silver/blue stripe background paper. She cut an 11½"x7⅞" piece of silver/blue tile paper. For the photo and the gemstone areas she cut a 5¼"x7¾" window and punched a square in the bottom-right and upper-left corners of the tile paper. For the photo frame Shauna used the cut out tile rectangle and measured ½" from each side, cut out the center and matted it on silver with a 1/16" border on each side of the frame. The photo was triple-matted: on silver, tiles then on silver again. The photo was attached to white vellum, the frame around it and the outer border of vellum trimmed to ¼". The picture was set off by gemstones. Shauna attached the photo to the page with foam tape, centered over the background window so the stripes show through the vellum. For the small squares Shauna used the punched out shapes, measured ¼" from each edge then cut out the inner square, leaving a frame. She matted each frame on silver with 1/16" borders on each side of the frame, then on vellum with ¼" borders. She attached these with foam tape over the background windows then added the large gemstones. The 11½"x3¼" vellum strip was attached to the page with eyelets and Shauna journaled with the black pen. For the crowning glory—sparkly letters. She die-cut the letters out of the tacky sheet, peeled off the backing and covered them with beads.

- **specialty Paper Pizazz™:** metallic silver/blue stripe, metallic silver/blue tile, metallic silver (*Metallic Silver*), white vellum (*Vellum Papers,* also by the sheet)
- **2" school house die-cut letters:** Accu/Cut®
- **sky blue glitter:** Art Accents™
- **Caribbean glass bead mix:** Micro Mosaics
- **gemstones:** Westrim Crafts
- **1¾" square punch:** Marvy® Uchida
- **1/8" silver eyelets:** Stamp Studio
- **black, silver pen:** Sakura Micron
- **Terrifically Tacky sheet:** Art Accents™
- **adhesive foam tape:** Therm O Web
- **designer:** Shauna Berglund-Immel

Sweet and simple, this page captures a fall day at the pumpkin patch in a traditional style. Lisa cut a 12"x8" piece of tan vellum then tore one 12" edge. She cut two 7" squares, one from ivory vellum and one from white vellum. She outlined the ivory with a gold pen and the white with copper. The photo was matted on sepia paper then on tan. She held the vellums in place with a stroke of glue in the center of the page. She cut three leaves from the paper and glued them to the background sheet. The torn vellum sheet was placed even with the bottom edge of the page and dots of glue on top of the leaves hold it in place. Finally the photo was glued centered on the page with gold journaling below.

- **patterned Paper Pizazz™:** brown & lace collage (*Pretty Collage Papers*), fall leaves (available by the sheet)
- **vellum Paper Pizazz™:** tan (*Colored Vellum Papers*), ivory (available by the sheet), white (*Vellum Papers,* also by the sheet)
- **solid Paper Pizazz™:** sepia, tan (*Solid Jewel Tones*)
- **gold, copper pens:** Sakura Gelly Roll
- **designer:** Lisa Garcia-Bergstedt

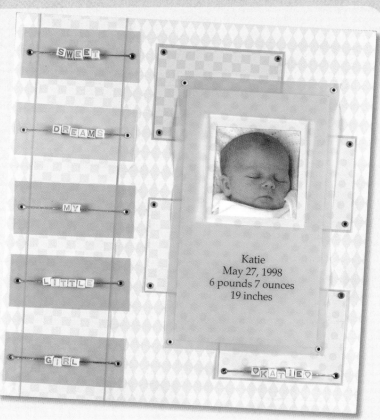

This refreshing page shows that vellum can give depth as well as transparency. Lisa started with a yellow diamond background. She cut a 2¾"x12" piece of pink checks, matted it on peach vellum and attached it 1" from the left edge. She cut five 4"x1½" pieces of different colored vellum and attached them evenly spaced over the pink checks with coordinating eyelets. For the photo, she cut a 4½"x8" piece of lavender dot and used the template to cut out a window. After computer journaling on yellow vellum, she placed it over the dot paper, and cut out a window ¾" larger and the whole piece 1" larger than the dot. Lisa cut four 4"x2⅞" pieces of different colored checks and dots papers and matted them on coordinating vellums. She attached them to the page with eyelets and attached the photo in the center. For the finishing touch, Lisa used letter beads strung on embroidery floss to spell out her message and Katie's name.

- **patterned Paper Pizazz**™: green checks, lavender dots, pink checks, aqua dots, yellow diamonds (*Soft Florals & Patterns*)
- **vellum Paper Pizazz**™: cornflower blue, yellow, peach, sage green, aqua (*Pastel Vellum Papers*)
- **Paper Flair**™ **Windows #1 template**
- **colored embroidery floss:** DMC
- **⅛" colored eyelets:** Stamp Studio
- **Alpha beads:** Darice
- **designer:** Lisa Garcia-Bergstedt

A day at the coast is perfectly captured in this innovative page. Shauna used computer journaling on tan vellum then tore the edges to mimic the soft lines and textures of the seashore. First she layed tan vellum over the lighthouse collage background and tore a strip across the bottom that followed the line of the shell border. She then turned it around and attached it to the top of the paper. She chalked vellum Cut-out™ seashells and added them to the vellum. The photo was matted on tan paper. Shauna made the ½" wide frame from tan vellum and attached it at an angle to draw your eye right to the photo. She used the template and tan vellum for the mini envelope, then filled it with vellum seashell Cut-outs™. By chalking the torn edges, frame and envelope, Shauana added depth and texture.

- **patterned Paper Pizazz**™: lighthouse collage (*Vacation Collage Papers*)
- **vellum Paper Pizazz**™: ivory (available by the sheet), tan (*Colored Vellum Papers,* also by the sheet)
- **solid Paper Pizazz**™: tan (*Solid Muted Colors*)
- **Paper Pizazz Cut-outs**™: shells (*Vellum Cut-outs*)
- **Paper Flair**™ **Mini Envelopes #1 Template**
- **black, brown decorating chalks:** Craf-T Products
- **black pen:** Sakura Micron
- **designer:** Shauna Berglund-Immel

Let it snow! This page delights in winter fun with layers and pockets of vellum. Lisa matted the photo on blue and added silver penwork. Then she matted it on white. She cut a piece of snowflake vellum to fit the width of the photo and to hang ½" over the top and bottom. She cut a window to highlight Cosmo, added silver penwork then attached it to the page with square eyelets. She enlarged a second photo on a color copier to 3½"x10½" and cut snowflake vellum to the same size. She inserted an eyelet above each corner and threaded the fibers on the page. For the letter "pockets" Lisa cut five 4½"x1½" strips of white vellum, folded them in half, tore the top front edge and chalked. She cut the letters from navy paper and matted them on white. She put a letter inside each "pocket" with a punched white snowflake then attached them to the page with blue eyelets. She finished with page by journaling with the black pen.

- **patterned Paper Pizazz**™: winter (*Holidays & Seasons Collage Papers*)
- **vellum Paper Pizazz**™: white (*Vellum Papers,* also by the sheet), white snowflakes (available by the sheet)
- **solid Paper Pizazz**™: blue, navy blue (*Solid Jewel Tones*), white (*Plain Pastel Papers*)
- **blue eyelets:** Stamp Studio

- **square silver eyelets:** Making Memories™
- **fibers:** Adornaments™
- **blue decorating chalk:** Craf-T Products
- **"fat lower" letter template:** Frances Meyer, Inc.
- **snowflake punch:** Marvy® Uchida
- **pens (black Micron, silver Gelly Roll):** Sakura
- **designer:** Lisa Garcia-Bergstedt

We love computer journaling on vellum—it's so easy! Lisa used three vellum blocks to tell the story of this friendship. She cut two 6" squares of the swirl paper and matted both on white. She placed them in opposite corners on the check paper to make quadrants. She matted the photo on white and journaled with the black pen. She cut eight 1½" white squares and two 3½" purple squares. She placed four white squares on each purple square leaving a narrow border between them. She punched eight hands from multiple colors and attached one to a white square with small flower eyelets. Lisa computer journaled on white vellum and cut each to 4½" square. Then she attached them to the page with large flower eyelets.

- **patterned Paper Pizazz**™: hot pink checks, hot pink swirls (*12"x12" Bright Tints*)
- **vellum Paper Pizazz**™: white (*Vellum Papers,* also by the sheet)
- **solid Paper Pizazz**™: white (*Solid Pastel Papers*), purple, green, yellow, blue (*Plain Brights*)
- **small, large flower eyelets:** Making Memories™
- **hand print punch:** McGill, Inc.
- **black pen:** Sakura Micron
- **designer:** Lisa Garcia-Bergstedt

Love blooms on this fun fall page! Arlene cut a 7½"x12" piece of tan flowered paper and matted it on tan vellum. She placed in on the right side of the ivory flowered background paper. She cut a 10½"x8¼" piece of flowered vellum and matted it on white vellum, tan vellum and ivory vellum. She highlighted the edges of each paper with the gold pen and attached the group to the page with gold snaps. Arlene matted both photos on gold paper and computer journaled on tan vellum then matted it on gold paper. She cut two 13" lengths of each fiber, twisted them together and placed them on the right side of the page, taping the ends to the back.

- **patterned Paper Pizazz™:** ivory flowered, tan flowered, tan flowered vellum (*Flowered "Handmade" Papers and Vellums*)
- **specialty Paper Pizazz™:** tan vellum (*Pastel Vellum Papers,* also by the sheet), white (*Vellum Papers,* also by the sheet, ivory (available by the sheet), metallic gold (*Metallic Gold,* also by the sheet)
- **yellow, brown fibers:** Adornaments™
- **gold snaps:** Making Memories™
- **gold pen:** Pentel of America, Ltd.
- **designer:** Arlene Peterson

Vacation memories captured in stitches and vellum pockets! Arlene cut green vellum ¼" smaller than the green leaf background paper. She cut leaf vellum to 6½"x11½", tore the right edge, placed it on the left side of the green vellum and whip stitched the two together with floss. She matted each photo on green paper then placed them on the page. She cut two 5"x2" and one 5¼"x2" piece of vellum for the pockets. She used a straight stitch and floss on three sides of each. Arlene place the two smaller pockets on top of the photos on the right and the larger on the left. She computer journaled on white vellum, stitched all four sides and placed it under the photo on the left. She added five buttons bringing dimension and interest to the page.

- **patterned Paper Pizazz™:** green leaf, green leaf vellum (*Joy's Garden*)
- **vellum Paper Pizazz™:** pastel green (*12"x12" Pastel Vellum Papers,* also by the sheet), white (*Vellum Papers,* also by the sheet)
- **solid Paper Pizazz™:** green (*Solid Muted Colors*)
- **green embroidery floss:** DMC
- **leaf buttons:** Dress It Up
- **designer:** Arlene Peterson

3-D & Lumpy

They're lumpy. They're bumpy. They're three-dimensional layouts—pages decorated with eyelets, buttons, fibers, charms and tags—just about anything else we scrappers can get our hands on!

How can you create great layouts with lumpy accents? We've got the answers, from Lisa's bathing suits hanging on a line (page 60) to Arlene's fun stitching techniques (page 65) and Shauna's playfull alphabet cut-outs!

While it's great fun to add these three-dimensional embellishments to a page, it is important to take precautions so your lumpy accents don't harm your precious photos. Plan your double-page spreads so a lumpy embellishment isn't directly opposite the photo on the facing page. Always use sheet protectors, so wire, eyelets and other metal items don't come in direct contact with photos. And be sure to store your albums upright.

Whether you're a veteran Lumpy Scrapper, or just bought your first package of eyelets, here are 19 designer lumpy layouts guaranteed to inspire your creative spirit!

Dress up—it's a favorite game for many young girls. What better way to capture those memories than this darling page?

1 A ½"x12" floral strip was attached to each side of the lavender textured background sheet.

2 Lisa began with four papers designed to work together. She followed the golden rule (see page 13) and matted the photos on white with a ⅟₃₂" border, then on three different patterned papers with ¼" borders. She attached one photo to the page with one layer of foam tape, the second with two layers and the third with three layers. By overlapping the photos Lisa created a "gallery" effect.

6 White penwork around the Austrian stones added the finishing, shining touch.

Molly

Buttons and bows, ribbons and curls, giggles and smiles, these are the things that little girls are made of!

5 Austrian stones at each corner of the vellum make this page sparkle.

4 The patterns on page 140 were used to make the purses, and Lisa put foam tape inside each one for depth. Notice the purses are made from coordinating papers. A button, stone and brad complete each lumpy purse.

3 She journaled on a 9½"x2½" piece of vellum and glued it to the page. Letting the purses separate the journaling is a nice touch.

- **patterned Paper Pizazz™:** floral, pink gingham, lavender floral, lavender textured (*Mixing Baby Papers*)
- **vellum Paper Pizazz™:** white (*Vellum Papers*, also by the sheet)
- **solid Paper Pizazz™:** white (*Solid Pastel Papers*)
- **Austrian stones:** Aurora Borealis, Dress It Up

- **pink button:** Dress It Up
- **³⁄₁₆" gold brad:** HyGlo/American Pin
- **adhesive foam tape:** Therm O Web
- **black pen:** Sakura Micron
- **white pen:** Pentel Gelly Roll
- **designer:** Lisa Garcia-Bergstedt

Sugar and spice and everything nice! Lisa made this black and white photo Fabulous with pretty patterned papers. She tore a 2½" strip of the checks paper and placed it on the right edge of the background. She journaled in green pen on a ¾"x12" piece of floral vellum and attached it over the checks. Lisa added interest when she offset the main elements of the page. She cut a 5" square of floral vellum and double-matted it on small floral and white. She placed it on point with the right corner over the checks and under the vellum. She matted the photo on white and purple then journaled with the black pen on the floral vellum. She cut out five large flowers, two small flowers and six sets of leaves. She attached the flowers to the page with foam tape and the leaves with glue dots. Fabulous fun with floral paper!

- **patterned Paper Pizazz**™: lavender/green companion papers (*Joy's Soft Collection*)
- **solid Paper Pizazz**™: white (*Solid Pastel Papers*), purple (*Solid Jewel Tones*)
- **adhesive foam tape:** Therm O Web
- **adhesive dots:** Glue Dots™
- **green, black pen:** Sakura
- **designer:** Lisa Garcia-Bergstedt

Arlene used the blue in Amanda's dress and shoes as inspiration for this sparkling page. She matted a 10"x10½" stripe paper on vellum and offset both on the floral background. She matted a 1½"x10½" silver strip on a 1½"x10½" vellum and placed in on the left side of the stripe paper. Arlene cut the out the tags and glued tiny silver marbles in the center of each flower. She matted each tag on silver paper, inserted an eyelet in the top of the two small ones and threaded fibers through the eyelets. Computer journaling on torn blue vellum completed the tags and compliments the page. She quadruple-matted the photo on silver, vellum, floral (she cut the paper from behind the stripe paper) and silver again. She added punched vellum and silver floral "photo corners" then glued seed beads to the center of each silver flower. Such a pretty page!

- **patterned Paper Pizazz**™: blue stripe, blue floral (*Jacie's Watercolor Naturals*)
- **specialty Paper Pizazz**™: pastel blue vellum (*12"x12" Pastel Vellum Papers*, also by the sheet), metallic silver (*Metallic Silver*)
- **Paper Pizazz**™ **Cut-Outs**™: *Tag Art #2*
- **blue seed beads:** Blue Moon Beads/Elizabeth Ward & Co., Inc.
- **tiny silver glass marbles:** Halcraft
- **⅛" silver eyelets:** Stamp Studio
- **blue and white fibers:** Adornaments™
- **½", 1" daisy punch:** Family Treasures, Inc.
- **adhesive foam tape:** Therm O Web
- **designer:** Arlene Peterson

Congratulations to Kimbery Llorens—our 1st place winner in the Oh Baby! page contest. She tore the bottom 1½" from an 11¼"10½" piece of light purple cardstock and placed them on the blue background paper. Kimberly tore twenty 2" squares of patterned paper to create the grid. She threaded buttons with floss and placed them on the yellow squares. She computer journaled words on white vellum then matted them on blue. Kimberly copied the photo onto vellum, then matted it on yellow with the photo corners. For "Gabriel" she stamped each letter on white with black ink, then matted them on the patterned papers. She embossed the footprints on white paper, then daubed blue ink on them and the letters. Kimberly connected the name with the rest of the page by stiching them together with fiber. She cut computer journaling on vellum to fit the tag, then threaded it with the ribbon. What a clever, sweet page!

- **patterned Paper Pizazz**™: yellow squiggle (*Soft Tints*), dark blue paisley, blue stripe (*Muted Tints*)
- **vellum Paper Pizazz**™: white (*Vellum Papers,* also by the sheet)
- **solid cardstock:** yellow, blue, light purple
- **½" wide sheer light blue ribbon:** C.M. Offray & Son, Inc.
- **buttons:** Dress It Up
- **fiber:** Adornaments™
- **metal rimmed tag:** Making Memories™

- **brass footprint embossing template:** Lasting Impressions
- **letter stamps:** Rubber Stampede, Inc.
- **blue, black ink:** Colorbox®
- **white photo corners:** Canson-Talens, Inc.
- **¾" square punch:** Marvy® Uchida
- **foam adhesive tape:** Therm O Web
- **photography:** Raclene Eckert
- **designer:** Kimberly Llorens

This page couldn't be cuter! The yellow swirl paper picks up on the gold highlights in Griffin's hair as well as the essence of summer—sun! Lisa matted the photo on white, yellow swirl and black. She used the patterns on page 142 to cut out the bathing suits and towel. The suits were matted on white—with foam tape in between—to add dimension. The grass came alive when trimmed with the deckle scissors. Cursive journaling finished the page.

- **patterned Paper Pizazz**™: clouds, grass, yellow swirl, teal swirl, rose paisley tile, rose floral (by the sheet), lavender stripe (*Muted Tints*)
- **solid Paper Pizazz**™: white (*Solid Pastel Papers*)
- **light brown Twistel**™: Making Memories™
- **tiny spring clothespins:** Forster Mfg, Inc.
- **letter templates:** Frances Meyer, Fat Caps upper and lower case
- **deckle decorative scissors:** Family Treasures, Inc.
- **adhesive foam tape:** Therm O Web
- **black pen:** Sakura Micron
- **designer:** Lisa Garcia-Bergstedt

The clever use of vellum windows gives this page unexpected depth, while the ribbon roses are a soft contrast to the squares and rectangles. Lisa cut a 4"x9" piece of solid yellow, then divided it into three rectangles: one 4"x2½", and two 4"x2¾". She cut a 1½" square window from one larger rectangle and glued the bride's picture to the back. She highlighted the first initial of the bride's new name with a window in the vellum. For the large photo: A 5¾"x8¼" yellow rectangle was cut with a 3¾" square window. After journaling, she carefully tore the bottom edge. Lisa overlayed vellum on each rectangle with ¼" excess on each edge. The leaves were made by cutting a 6" length of green ribbon with deep inverted "V's" in each end. The center was gathered and sewn to the page. The roses were made with a 6" peach ribbon length. One end was sewn to the page and then wrapped around itself and the end sewn under the flower. The charm was strung on peach thread and hung from the roses.

- **patterned Paper Pizazz™:** yellow dots on green (*Mixing Heritage Papers*)
- **vellum Paper Pizazz™:** yellow (*Pastel Vellum Papers,* also by the sheet)
- **solid Paper Pizazz™:** yellow (*Solid Muted Colors*)
- **½" wide peach wire-edge, 2" wide green satin ribbon:** C.M. Offray & Son, Inc.
- **gold heart charm:** S. Axelrod Co.
- **peach thread, needle**
- **black pen:** Sakura Micron
- **designer:** Lisa Garcia-Bergstedt

(see the companion page on page 126)

Yum! Lisa was inspired by Emma's voracious appetite when creating this page. She matted the photo on white then on red. The red die-cut letters really pop off the page once she matted them on white and attached them with foam tape. She cut a pile of pasta with one strand coming up then matted it on white. The fork was cut from silver paper using the pattern on page 140. Then the noodle was wrapped around the tines, linking the elelments together. After mounting the letters and journaling, she wrapped Twistel™ around the letters to tie in the pasta on the bottom of the page.

- **patterned Paper Pizazz™:** spaghetti (*Yummy Papers,* also by the sheet), red plaid (by the sheet)
- **specialty Paper Pizazz™:** silver (*Metallic Silver,* also by the sheet)
- **solid Paper Pizazz™:** red (*Solid Jewel Tones*), white (*Solid Pastel Papers*)
- **schoolhouse die-cut letters:** Accu/Cut® Systems
- **yellow Twistel™:** Making Memories™
- **adhesive foam tape:** Therm O Web
- **black pen:** Sakura Micron
- **designer:** Lisa Garcia-Bergstedt

Tiny toes and a sweet face were the precious inspirations for this page. Lisa cropped and matted the photos on white, then on blue textured paper. For the page title she journaled on white vellum then matted on blue. Turning it at an angle added interest and draws the eye right to the photo! The text blocks were journaled on white then matted on yellow. For the marbles, Lisa journaled on yellow and blue paper, then glued the paper to the flat sides and onto the page with glue dots. What an effective way to highlight your feelings about the little one.

- **patterned Paper Pizazz™:** yellow dots, blue textured (*Mixing Baby Papers*)
- **vellum Paper Pizazz™:** white (*Vellum Papers,* also by the sheet)
- **solid Paper Pizazz™:** yellow (*Solid Pastel Papers*)
- **clear flat-back marbles:** Panacea
- **black pen:** Sakura Micron
- **tacky craft glue:** Aleene's
- **glue dots:** Glue Dots™
- **designer:** Lisa Garcia-Bergstedt

Swirls, twirls and a cute little girl—that's what this page is made of. Lisa cut a 3"x12" and a 2½"x12" strip of light tan, tore and chalked the edges then added them to the left side of the page. She matted the photo on tan and brown then attached it with foam tape. She computer journaled on light tan then matted it on brown and attached it with foam tape. She cut a ⅞"x5⅜" piece of tan and matted it on brown. Then she inserted an eyelet in each end. She made a coil from each color of wire by wrapping the wire tightly on a round toothpick. She threaded them on another piece, securing them on the back. She attached it with foam tape. Lisa made seven wire swirls of alternating colors and placed them on the photo corners, the light tan border and as a picture hanger. She journaled Holland's name with the black pen to add balance and weight to the left side.

- **patterned Paper Pizazz™:** brown swirls (*Great Backgrounds*)
- **solid Paper Pizazz™:** light tan (*Solid Pastel Papers*), tan, brown (*Solid Jewel Tones*)
- **natural, copper, brown wire:** Artistic Wire, Ltd.
- **copper eyelets:** Stamp Studio
- **light brown decorating chalks:** Craf-T Products
- **black pen:** Sakura Micron
- **adhesive foam tape:** Therm O Web
- **designer:** Lisa Garcia-Bergstedt

To cherish: 1.To have highest regard for; to recognize the worth, quality, importance of. 2. To hold dear.

Congratulations to Kimbery Llorens—our Honorable Mention winner in the Oh Baby! page contest. She wove this winner with 1" strips of patterned paper for the background. She wrapped each corner in 1" wide satin ribbon and taped them to the back to secure. Kimberly cut a 3¼"x8¼" piece of mint green paper and matted it on pink. She computer journaled on white vellum, embossed the footprints and tore the edges. She stiched the papers together in each corner with pink floss. She tied a bow with sheer ribbon and glued a ribbon rose to the center. In place of paper, Kimberly edged the photo with ³⁄₁₆" wide satin ribbon and matted it on a 5¼"x7¼" piece of pink vellum. She outlined the vellum with gold to help it pop off the background. Eight ribbon roses accent the mat like the flowers on her dress. A fun and interesting page—great job Kimberly!

- **patterned Paper Pizazz™:** pink posies (*12"x12" Soft Tints*), green with white dots, tiny pink rose buds (*Mixing Soft Patterned Papers*)
- **vellum Paper Pizazz™:** white (*Vellum Papers,* also by the sheet), pastel pink (*12"x12" Pastel Vellum Papers,* also by the sheet)
- **solid Paper Pizazz™:** light pink, mint green (*Solid Pastel Papers*)
- **¼" wide sheer pink, ³⁄₁₆", 1" wide pink satin ribbons:** C.M. Offray & Son, Inc.
- **ribbon roses:** The Card Connection™
- **pink decorating chalk:** Craf-T Products
- **brass footprint embossing template:** Lasting Impressions
- **pink embroidery floss:** DMC
- **gold pen:** Sakura Gelly Roll
- **designer:** Kimberly Llorens

Shauna "puzzled" this page together with fantastic results! For the title she tore a 10½"x3½" piece of tan vellum then overlayed a 9½"x2½" piece of ivory vellum. She attached them to the page with gold eyelets. Shauna used the puzzle piece die-cuts (see page 141 for patterns) to highlight each person from an extra group photo. She tore a 6" ivory vellum heart and a 4½" tan vellum heart. She cut out the letters from *Alphabet Tiles.* Shauna computer journaled on ivory and tan vellum then tore the edges. She matted the photo on gold. Once she liked the layout she attached some elements directly on the page and others with foam tape. You win Shauna!

- **patterned Paper Pizazz™:** brown collage (*Masculine Collage Papers*)
- **specialty Paper Pizazz™:** white vellum (*Vellum Papers,* also by the sheet), tan vellum (*Pastel Vellum Papers,* also by the sheet, ivory vellum (by the sheet), metallic gold (*Metallic Gold,* also by the sheet)
- **alphabet cut-outs:** Artsy Collage™ Alphabet Tiles
- **puzzle pieces die-cuts:** Accu/Cut® Systems
- **⅛" gold eyelets:** Stamp Studio
- **adhesive foam tape:** Therm O Web
- **photography:** I.N.V.U. Portraits by Helen
- **designer:** Shauna Berglund-Immel

(see the companion page on page 129)

Monochromatic papers make this use of vellum masculine and magic. Paris computer journaled on vellum and tore it to 3"x9". She attached it to the background over the black pen "Mount Hood" journaling with an eyelet in each corner. She matted the photo on vellum, the companion paper and a 7"x9" piece of torn vellum. She tore a 7"x2" piece of vellum and attached it under the photo with one eyelet in each end. She shaped the paper wire into a zig-zag and threaded it through the eyelets. Paris cut two road signs from the companion paper and attached each to a vellum tag. She threaded the tags onto Twistel™ and attached them to the page with foam tape. She used the black pen to journal at the bottom of the page. What a ride!

- **patterned Paper Pizazz™:** road sign collage companion papers (*Vacation Collage*)
- **vellum Paper Pizazz™:** pastel green (*12"x12" Pastel Vellum Papers,* also by the sheet)
- **dark green paper wrapped wire:** Paper Reflections® DMD Industries
- **vellum tags, sage green Twistel™, square pewter eyelets:** Making Memories™ Details™
- **black pen:** Zig Writer
- **adhesive foam tape:** Therm O Web
- **designer:** Paris Dukes

Arlene captured the strong beauty of the Smokey Mountains in this rugged page. She tore a 3"x12" strip of green/tan stripe paper for the top border. She cut a 2¼"x6¾" piece of animal/tree check paper and triple-matted it on white, sponged and white again. She placed an eyelet in each corner and threaded the wire through, spiraling each end. For the bottom border Arlene cut three 1½"x2½" sponged rectangles, two 1"x2½" stripe rectangles and two 1"x2½" animal/tree rectangles. She cut the tops and bottoms of each at an angle and matted them on white paper. Arlene placed an eyelet in each corner then threaded the wire through, spiraling the ends. She triple-matted the photo on white, animal/tree, and white again. She cut a 2¼"x4½" piece of animal/tree paper and matted it on white. Arlene computer journaled on white vellum. She cut a park service sign from a photo and placed it next to the title. She capped off the page with animal and tree buttons.

- **patterned Paper Pizazz™:** green/tan stripe, animal/tree check, pinecone, brown sponged (*Mixing Masculine Papers*)
- **vellum Paper Pizazz™:** white (*Vellum Papers,* also by the sheet)
- **white eyelets:** Stamp Studio
- **white wire:** Artistic Wire Ltd.
- **tree, deer, bear buttons:** Dress It Up
- **designer:** Arlene Peterson

Arlene added lumps and bumps to this delightful page with embroidery floss. For the top border she cut three 1¾"x2¾" star stripes rectangles and two 2¼"x1¾" check rectangles. She matted each on blue paper then stitched them to the background paper with floss. Arlene used a 1"x11" piece of scrap paper behind the border to hold all the pieces together. She computer journaled on vellum then punched out each word with the 1½" punch. She punched five 1" blue stars, placed one behind each vellum star and attached them to the page with Glue Dots™. For the bottom border Arlene computer journaled on vellum and cut it to 4¼"x1¼" then matted it on star stripes and blue then stitched them together. She cut two 1¾" check squares, punched three ½" stars from each and matted the squares on blue. She punched two 1½" vellum stars and four ½" blue stars. She layered a blue star on each vellum star then attached them to the squares with Glue Dots™. She placed two ½" check stars and one blue star at each side of the journaling. Arlene matted the photo on five papers—blue, check, white, star stripes and blue again. She unifed the page by stitching the mats together. So sweet!

- **patterned Paper Pizazz™:** blue moon & stars, yellow/blue check, blue & yellow star stripes (*Mixing Baby Papers*)
- **vellum Paper Pizazz™:** pastel yellow (*12"x12" Pastel Vellum Papers,* also by the sheet)
- **solid Paper Pizazz™:** light blue (*Plain Pastels*)
- **½", 1", 1½" star punches:** Marvy® Uchida
- **yellow, blue embroidery floss:** DMC
- **adhesive glue dots:** Glue Dots™
- **designer:** Arlene Peterson

Lisa captures the excitement of the day a college acceptance letter arrives! The cloud background paper reflects a young girl's dreams, while it is an appropriate setting for the ivy and mailbox. She cropped and matted the photo on white then on black. She cut the 1⅝"x8" mailbox post from barnwood paper and cut out leaves from the ivy paper. Notice she cut some individual leaves—and mounted them with foam tape—while others are in groups. Using the pattern on page 141, Lisa cut the mailbox from silver and black papers, then pieced it together on top of the post. She used a brad to fasten the flag to the box. She put Sara's name on with sticker letters and inserted the envelope and letter inside.

- **patterned Paper Pizazz™:** stamps, clouds, barnwood, ivy (by the sheet)
- **specialty Paper Pizazz™:** metallic silver, (*Metallic Silver,* also by the sheet)
- **solid Paper Pizazz™:** red, black (*Solid Jewel Tones*)
- **⅛" silver brad:** HyGlo/American Pin
- **black sticker letters:** Déjà Views®
- **adhesive foam tape:** Therm O Web
- **black pen:** Sakura Micron
- **designer:** Lisa Garcia-Bergstedt

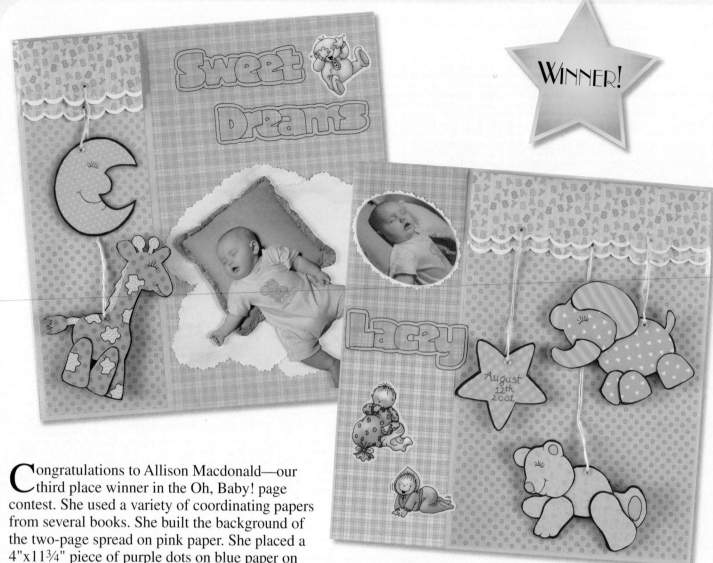

Congratulations to Allison Macdonald—our third place winner in the Oh, Baby! page contest. She used a variety of coordinating papers from several books. She built the background of the two-page spread on pink paper. She placed a 4"x11¾" piece of purple dots on blue paper on the left page and balanced it with a 7¾"x11¾" piece on the right page. In the middle she placed a 7½"x12" piece of purple plaid on the left page and a 3¾"x12" piece on the right page. For the "curtain" on each page she cut an 11¾"x2" piece and an 11¾"x2½" piece of "BABY" paper. She used the seagull template to scallop one long edge of each and matted them on white. She cut 4" from each and inserted the eyelets. Allison mounted the curtains to the page with a layer of foam tape. She used the template to cut the letters from a pastel plaid paper, matted them on pink paper and added black penwork. She cut the main photo as a silhouette then made "clouds" with white paper and

ripple scissors—a little chalking added depth. She used the template to cut the small photo into an oval then matted it on white and trimmed it with the scissors. Allison strove for continuity and matted the stickers on pink paper then placed them on the pages. She thought of a way to have three-dimensonal elements hang from her page and still be protected. She made double-sided paper pieces, inserted an eyelet in each then laminated them! She punched holes in the sheet protectors and tied the paper pieces to the eyelets in the curtains with embroidery floss! Great idea and great pages Allison!

- **patterned Paper Pizazz**™: "BABY" (*Mixing Baby Papers*), purple dots on blue (*Mixing Soft Patterned Papers*), white hearts on mint green (*Stripes, Checks & Dots*), purple stripes, yellow/pink gingham, pink posies on yellow, purple dots on lavender, yellow squiggles (*Soft Tints*), white dots on peach (*Making Heritage Scrapbook Pages*)
- **solid Paper Pizazz**™: mint green, pink (*Plain Pastels*)
- **Paper Pizazz**™ **stickers:** baby in yellow (*Annie Lang's Baby*), baby in green, crawling baby (*Annie Lang's Baby #2*)
- **Paper Pizazz**™ **cut-outs:** moon, giraffe, bear, elephant (*201 Paper Piecing Patterns*)

- **pink, yellow, green, peach, purple eyelets:** Stamp Studio
- **pink, yellow, green, peach, purple embroidery floss:** DMC
- **light blue chalk:** Craf-T Products
- **Fat Caps, Fat Lower letter templates:** Francis Meyer, Inc.
- **star, seagull border templates:** Making Memories™
- **ripple pattern edge scissors, oval template:** Fiskars®
- **⅛" hole punch:** Marvy® Uchida
- **laminate sheets:** Xyron™
- **adhesive foam tape:** Therm O Web
- **designer:** Allison Macdonald

Imagine the treasures to be found in Mom's Sunday dress collection. Lisa created this pretty page by using two coordinated blue papers with a black & white photograph. She matted the photo on white paper, on blue floral paper and white again to make the floral paper pop off the diamonds. After attaching the photo to the center of the page, Lisa journaled around it. She computer journaled on a 5¼"x2¾" piece of white paper. For the darling dresses she used the pattern on page 144 to fold the paper into the blouses and gathered 3" lengths of ribbon into the skirts. She used the pattern below to form the wire into two hangers then "hung" the shirts. Lisa mixed a simple cursive font with a fancy title to really highlight this page.

- **patterned Paper Pizazz™:** blue floral, blue diamonds, pink hydrangeas (*Mixing Soft Florals and Patterns*)
- **solid Paper Pizazz™:** white (*Solid Pastel Papers*)
- **2" wide ribbon:** C.M. Offray & Son, Inc.
- **22-gauge copper wire:** Artistic Wire Ltd.
- **adhesive foam tape:** Therm O Web
- **black pen:** Sakura Micron
- **designer:** Lisa Garcia-Bergstedt

Lynda Jane's
SUNDAY BEST

Lynda   *Jane*

1952

Mom always loved a new dress. By the time she was eleven she learned to sew and was making herself a new Sunday dress at least once a week. I have kept a few of the dresses that she made herself. This photo and those dresses will always remind me of how beautiful and talented she really is!

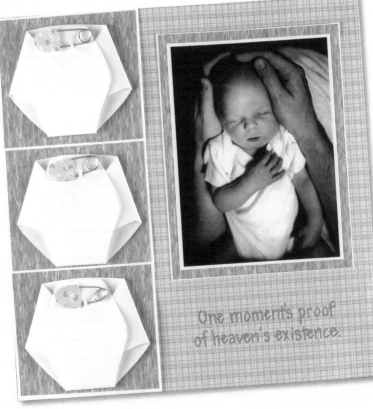

One moment's proof of heaven's existence.

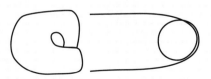

Emma
Louise
Camarda

inside

Sweet babies lead to sweet scrapbook pages. The photo was matted on white, pink strokes paper and on white again to keep the strokes paper from dissappearing into the plaid. For diapers, Lisa used the pattern on page 140 to cut three from white. She formed 3" lengths of wire into three diaper pin shapes, cut slits in the front flap of each diaper and threaded the wires through. She used the pin head pattern on yellow journaling paper then attached them with foam tape. She journaled the baby's name inside the top diaper, the birth date in the center and measurements in the bottom—each matted on stroke then on white. Behind the diapers, Lisa put a 4⅝"x12" white rectangle then three 4½"x3⅞" strokes rectangles.

- **patterned Paper Pizazz™:** pink plaid, pink strokes, yellow journaling (*Mixing Baby Papers*)
- **solid Paper Pizazz™:** white (*Solid Pastel Papers*)
- **20-gauge wire:** Artistic Wire Ltd.
- **adhesive foam tape:** Therm O Web
- **black pen, pink opaque pen:** Sakura Micron
- **designer:** Lisa Garcia-Bergstedt

I'm a scrapbook junkie! I've done over 35 scrapbooks!! When I was a new stay at home mom, scrapbooking was a savior. It introduced me to new friends and a way to keep my sanity! It helped me remember I was still a creative person underneath all of the new responsibilities as a mother. Now my daughter is 8 and scrapbooking is something we do together. She loves to look through the scrapbooks I've done. Grandma jokes that Natalie will be the most well-documented person when she becomes president some day!!

Paris

Our Scrapbook Specialists Share...

I know how much I cherish pictures of my mom and dad from when they were young and I want to be able to share my life and the people around me with my kids some day. It helps us to remember all the things we've done and also helps to remind us of what is truly important in life, the people in our lives. I've always loved being creative and I grew up taking pictures and putting them in albums, it's great that they can both come together. Scrapbooking is important to me to share our yesterdays, love today, and envision our tomorrows.

Toddi

Scrapbooking is my escape—you could say it's my therapy. I have met some of my best friends through scrapbooking! Scrapbooking is like a quilt or a journal—it's a truly unique hobby that links us on so many levels. I have great joy when my granddaughter Hailey asks me to read the stories from her album as a bed-time story. The joy on her face keeps me creating my own books and also helps me on a creative level.

Arlene

Paper, stories, photos...these are irresistible to me! I love writing, I love photos (the older, the better!) and I love the wonderful scrapbooking toys I get to play with! Best of all, scrapbooking gives me the chance to become a storyteller; I am lucky to have lots of photos, including heritage photos, and it's important to me that these people and their stories are documented and preserved in a way that honors who they were. And with scrapbooking, I can pass on a little piece of myself, too, so whoever looks at these albums in the future knows that my family is important to me.

Sara

... ways been into art and design. ... ing and using my imagination makes ... me. it's part of who i am. it runs in ... blood. it's my passion. i grew up with ... s and paper and scissors and i would ... re never imagined those things would ... ll be so prominent in my life today. it ... mbines my love of my family, photography ... nd art. i love the creative process. i love ... !!!! i can't get enough of it!!! it's therapy. ... rt therapy. it's just what the doctor ... ordered. to put ideas on paper is exhila- ... rating. it's freedom!

Shauna

Placing my photos in scrapbooks gives a more complete record of my family's life than if I just put those photos in frames. After my mother passed away, I inherited 3 large orange boxes of photos with no information about dates or other important facts about my family. What I would give for just a few scribbled notes on the backs of those photos. I want my daughter Lauren to have the most complete record I can give her of our family—so she can pass these memories down to her children.

LeNae

... t's the feeling. A page with heartfelt journaling that makes you melt when you read it and look at the photos...who could resist? Whether it's the feeling of pride when you do a great page or complete an album, or the happy or funny family memories that are triggered when you look through your scrapbook (by yourself or with your kids, telling them all about things they did when they were little, which makes more happy memories!), or the sentimental feelings of leaving something for future generations to know something about their family heritage. It's giving a part of yourself that's unique, creative, heartfelt, and fun.

Susan

Heartfelt Journaling

"There are thousands of thoughts lying within a man that he does not know till he takes up the pen and writes." ~William Makepeace Thackeray

They say a picture is worth a thousand words. Yet those of us who've looked at photos from years past might wish for just a little more information. Who was that long-gone ancestor, staring out from a 1920 photo? This translates to how we scrapbook today. Ask yourself: What do I want to tell my great-grandchildren, who will surely treasure the scrapbooks I make today?

Journaling is often one of the most intimidating aspects of scrapbooking. Maybe it's because we don't like our handwriting. Maybe we worry about our grammar, spelling or punctuation. Maybe we don't feel confident in our ability to say just the right thing.

Heartfelt journaling is different. It takes away the handwriting issue, the writer's block, the fear of the grade-school grammar teacher. Heartfelt journaling is simply this: say what is in your heart, and know that what you say in your scrapbook—regardless of your handwriting, your grammar, your spelling—will be a treasure to those who will pore over your scrapbooks in the years to come.

Sometimes you just need some inspiration. On the next few pages, our Scrapbook Specialists take up the topic of Heartfelt Journaling with 12 examples of great layouts that will inspire you to take your pen in hand (or maybe sit down in front of your computer) and try a little heartfelt journaling of your own.

Happy Birthday USA! Lisa spells out patriotism on this American page. She cut the flag from its background and matted it on stars on navy paper. She matted the photo on navy and glued it to the stripes of the flag. She cut out the tag art letters and matted each on navy. She tied the buttons to the letters with white floss then attached them to 1½" white squares matted on navy. She cut a 1¾"x8½" white vellum rectangle and an oval from yellow vellum for the candle and flame. She crumpled both then flatted them before attaching them to the page. Notice the red floss stitched between them. She stitched the metal numbers on with red buttons and white floss. Lisa computer journaled patriotic feelings on white vellum then cut out each word and attached them with eyelets. She journaled with black pens. A page to salute!

- **patterned Paper Pizazz™:** stars on navy, American flag (both available by the sheet), tags (*Tag Art*, also available by the sheet)
- **vellum Paper Pizazz™:** white (*Velllum Papers,* also by the sheet), yellow (*Pastel Vellum Papers,* also available by the sheet)
- **solid Paper Pizazz™:** navy (*Solid Jewel Tones*)
- **⅛" silver eyelets:** Stamp Studio
- **red, white embroidery floss:** DMC
- **metal number tags:** Making Memories® Details™ Tagged™
- **buttons:** Dress It Up
- **black pens:** Sakura Micron and Opaque
- **adhesive foam tape:** Therm O Web
- **designer:** Lisa Garcia-Bergstedt

A letter from the heart—this page tells the story of a mother's love. Lisa used photo tinting pens to color the teddy bear and Griffin's lips then matted it on white and dark blue. She computer journaled on white vellum, tore and chalked the edge. She stitched it to the page with cream floss, starting at the top left corner. For the picture hanger she threaded an 8" wire through the button then tucked the ends under the photo. The other button is simply threaded with wire then glued to the page. She used the black pen to journal the photo caption and to highlight certain words in her letter. This sweet page will be cherished for years.

- **patterned Paper Pizazz™:** tiny plaid (*Mixing Baby Papers*)
- **vellum Paper Pizazz™:** white (*Velllum Papers,* also by the sheet)
- **solid Paper Pizazz™:** white (*Plain Pastel Papers*), dark blue (*Solid Jewel Tones*)
- **heart buttons:** Making Memories™
- **cream embroidery floss:** DMC
- **silver wire:** Artistic Wire, Ltd.
- **blue decorating chalks:** Craf-T Products
- **black pen:** Sakura Micron
- **photo tinting pens (woodland, blush):** Zig® Photo Twins™
- **designer:** Lisa Garcia-Bergstedt

Grandmas are special and Paris perfectly captured the era of the photos in this vintage inspired page. She attached the photos to a 4"x7¾" piece of burgundy floral paper with photo corners then matted the whole piece on ivory. Paris cut a 4½"x8½" piece of stripe paper and matted it on ivory. She computer journaled the list on ivory vellum then tore it to 5½"x10." She overlayed the vellum on the stripe paper. For the title she tore a 12"x3½" strip of ivory vellum and journaled "Grandma" with the black pen. She journaled "Thank you…" on a 5"x1½" piece of torn white vellum. Paris attached the vellum pieces to the page, then hid the adhesive behind the buttons with Glue Dots™. A lovely memory Paris.

- **patterned Paper Pizazz**™: burgundy/white floral, burgundy/tan stripe, burgundy floral (*Joy's Vintage Papers*)
- **vellum Paper Pizazz**™: white (*Velllum Papers,* also by the sheet), ivory (by the sheet)
- **solid Paper Pizazz**™: ivory (*Plain Pastels*)
- **vintage brown/tan marbled buttons**
- **black photo corners:** Canson-Talens, Inc.
- **ivory embroidery floss:** DMC
- **black pen:** Jimmie Gel Rollerball
- **adhesive glue dots:** Glue Dots™
- **designer:** Paris Dukes

Daddy's little girl! Sweet memories and a darling photo capture the love of a daughter. Shauna trimmed lacy paper to 11" square then matted it on red and white trimmed with the scallop scissors. She matted the photo on white, red and white again trimmed with the scallop scissors. She inserted two white eyelets and strung the alphabet beads on the fiber. Shauna computer journaled childhood memories on white then highlighted key words with chalk. The whole piece was matted on red with a button tied with fiber. Shauna drew a red circle in each scallop bump on the page. What a way to make a page pop!

- **patterned Paper Pizazz**™: lace on red (*Lacy Papers*)
- **red, white 12"x12" cardstock**
- **white eyelets:** Stamp Studio
- **alpahbet beads:** Darice®
- **white fiber:** On The Surface Fibers
- **heart button:** Hill Creek Designs
- **red decorating chalk:** Craf-T Products
- **red pen:** Zig® Writer
- **glue dots:** Glue Dots™
- **scallop decorative scissors:** Fiskars®
- **designer:** Shauna Berglund-Immel

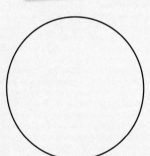

Across the miles this page is full of sisterly love. Lisa stamped on a 10" length of ribbon, tied it around the photo then matted it on black. She tore a 6"x5" and an 8"x4" piece of barnwood paper, chalked the edges and matted them on black with torn edges. She cut five letters from the letters paper, matted them on black and put two behind the photo. Lisa computer journaled individual words in different fonts on white, chalked and matted them on black. She used the envelope pattern on page 142 and letters paper, wrapped it with ribbon, matted it on black then glued it to the barnwood paper. She used the template below to cut the tag from white paper that she stamped and chalked. She matted it on silver then tied it to the ribbon with Twistel™. Lisa attached the large barnwood piece to the page with an eyelet in each corner, threaded them with Twistel™ and tucked the remaining three letters behind it. She inserted two eyelets on the left side of the page for the word strip, threaded Twistel™ and attached the words with foam tape. For the finishing touch she tore four stamps from the stamps paper, chalked the edges and glued them to the page.

- **patterned Paper Pizazz™:** crackle (*Spattered, Crackled, Sponged,* also available by the sheet), barnwood, letters, stamps (all available by the sheet)
- **specialty Paper Pizazz™:** metallic silver (*Metallic Silver,* also available by the sheet)
- **solid Paper Pizazz™:** black (*Solid Jewel Tones*), white (*Plain Pastel Papers*)
- **⅛" silver eyelets:** Stamp Studio

- **brown Twistel™:** Making Memories™
- **24" of ⅝" wide peach grosgrain ribbon:** C.M. Offray & Son, Inc.
- **brown deocorating chalk:** Craf-T Products
- **quote stamp, black ink pad:** Rubber Stampede, Inc.
- **adhesive foam tape:** Therm O Web
- **designer:** Lisa Garcia-Bergstedt

Happiness is… a whimical page like this one—full of sentiment. Lisa's glimpse of cousin fun started with the photo she quadruple-matted on tan, black, sprigs on black and finally on black again. She used computer journaling on tan paper and two fonts for the titles and sentiments. She cut out one each then matted them on white with hairline borders. Before she attached them to the page, she spent some time arranging them to find just the right fit. She used the patterns on page 140 for the hats and "hung" them with foam tape on the journaling block to tie in the hats in the photo.

- **patterned Paper Pizazz™:** black/white vine, sprigs on black (*Mixing Hertiage Papers*)
- **solid Paper Pizazz™:** black (*Solid Jewel Tones*), white (*Plain Pastel Papers*), tan (*Solid Muted Colors*)
- **adhesive foam tape:** Therm O Web
- **designer:** Lisa Garcia-Bergstedt

This delightful page celebrates young Griffin's individuality. Lisa kept it simple, yet fun with circles and stars. She matted the photo on black, light green and on black again. Lisa punched out two circles of each size in alternating vellum colors. For the text block, she computer journaled on light green paper. For Griffin's name she computer journaled on white vellum. She cut both to 6"x3¼" then matted them on black, dark green and on black again. She inserted a dark green eyelet in each vellum corner. Lisa used the black pen to journal some of the words in the text block onto the circles, then attached them to the page with alternating eyelet colors. For the finishing touch and depth she attached the text block and the photo to the page with foam tape.

- **patterned Paper Pizazz™:** stars on green (*Great Backgrounds*)
- **vellum Paper Pizazz™:** light green, green (*Pastel Vellum Papers*), white (*Vellum Papers,* also by the sheet)
- **solid Paper Pizazz™:** black, dark green (*Solid Jewel Tones*), light green (*Solid Muted Colors*)
- **⅛" light green, dark green eyelets:** Stamp Studio
- **2", 2½", 3" circle punches:** Marvy® Uchida
- **black pen:** Sakura Micron
- **adhesive foam tape:** Therm O Web
- **designer:** Lisa Garcia-Bergstedt

Paris used the beautiful rhododendron flowers for her color inspiration when building this page. She matted each photo on white then matted them together on a 9½"x6" piece of plaid then matted that on solid lavender. She cut a tiny tag, 1½"x¾," out of lavender and punched a hole in the top. She cut out the floral tag, inserted an eyelet then journaled on both tags with the black pen. Paris threaded fibers through the tags and attached them to the page with foam tape. For the border on the bottom of the page she cut a 12"x4" piece of plaid and overlayed a torn 12"x2" piece of vellum, attaching it with heart brads. Paris computer journaled on white paper, then cut out each phrase. She matted each on lavender and arranged them on the page.

- **patterned Paper Pizazz™:** lavender plaid, pastel lavender floral (*Joy's Soft Collection of Papers*), lavender floral tag (*Tag Art #2*)
- **solid Paper Pizazz™:** lavender (*Plain Pastels*)
- **purple fibers:** Adornments™
- **silver heart brads:** HyGlo/American Pin
- **silver eyelet:** Stamp Studio
- **⅛" hole punch:** McGill, Inc.
- **black pen:** Jimmie Gel Rollerball
- **adhesive foam tape:** Therm O Web
- **adhesive glue dots:** Glue Dots™
- **designer:** Paris Dukes

"Hula is the language of the heart, and therefore the heartbeat of the Hawaiian people."
-King David Kalakaua

Hawaii's

The beauty and drums of Tahiti... fast rhythmic movements and swishing grass skirts!

- **patterned Paper Pizazz™:** 12"x12" clouds, sandstone (both available by the sheet)
- **vellum Paper Pizazz™:** green (*12"x12" Pastel Vellum Papers,* also by the sheet)
- **multi-colored fibers:** Rubba Dub Dub Fibers
- **shells, starfish:** US Shell, Inc.
- **Paper Flair™ Tags template**
- **tiny letter tiles:** made in Australia
- **black, green decorating chalk:** Craf-T Products
- **South Seas stamps:** Art Accents by Postalz
- **circle punch:** McGill, Inc.
- **pop dots:** All Night Media®
- **mini, regular glue dots:** Glue Dots™
- **black pen:** Sakura Gelly Roll
- **designer:** Shauna Berglund-Immel

Hula—Shauna brings the islands home with this fun spread. She tore the top edges of two 12"x8" pieces of green vellum. She chalked each and layered them over the clouds background paper. She tore the top edges of two 12"x7" pieces of sandstone, chalked and layered them over the vellum. She cut four tags from cloud paper using the template then repeated the vellum and sandstone papers. Shauna added postage stamps to the tags with pop dots, then punched ½" vellum circles and glued them over the holes. She threaded 5" strands of fibers and glued the ends to the page. She journaled on four ¾" vellum squares, chalked and added them to the tags. The tiny letter tiles add journaling in a small space. She attached the tags with pop dots and the shells with Glue Dots™. She added shadow and definition to the tags by chalking the edges and the paper underneath. Shauna matted the photos on sandstone then vellum with chalked edges. She computer journaled on vellum then tore and chalked the edges. She completed the page with hand journaling. Pages to remember.

Shauna and Tasha The Polynesian Cultural Center Hawaii 1978

Art and Soul

Dances of the South Pacific have meaning beyond words. The graceful Hula is an integrated system of poetry, movement and rhythm. It is the literature of the Hawaiian People.

To watch Hula is to read a book about Hawaii. The dance is the interpretation of the words of a song and the method in which ancient Hawaiians passed along the stories and legends of their culture to subsequent generations.

Toddi fillled this page with memories of time spent with Mom! She matted the photo on white. She then tore a 4"x6" piece of white vellum and a 3"x7" piece of blue vellum and placed the photo on top. She tore a ¾"x8" strip of white vellum and a ¾"x6½" strip of blue vellum then placed them vertically on the page. Toddi tore five rectangles of blue velum: one 2¼"x1", one 2¾"x2", one 3½"x2", one 2¾"x2¼" and one 3½"x2¼". She attached them to the page with flower eyelets and journaled with the black pen. She inserted an eyelet in each corner of the background paper, threaded floss through each eyelet and tied a bow at the top of the page. What a fun way to dress up a special photo!

- **patterned Paper Pizazz™**: blue flowers collage (*Jacie & Joy's 8½"x11" Collage*)
- **vellum Paper Pizazz™: pastel** blue (*12"x12" Pastel Vellum Papers*, also by the sheet), white (*Vellum Papers,* also by the sheet)
- **light blue embroidery floss**: DMC
- **⅛" white flower eyelets:** Making Memories™
- **black pen:** Sakura Gelly Roll
- **designer:** Toddi Barclay

A fun page filled with swirls and twirls! Toddi triple-matted the photo on ivory, dark swirls and ivory again. She tore a 12"x2" strip and a 3½"x2½" rectangle from vellum. She added them to the top of the page with the photo. Toddi cut a 12"x2" strip of dark swirls and matted it on ivory. She placed it near the bottom of the page over a torn 12"x4½" piece of vellum. She shaped the wire into key words and incorporated them into the black pen journaling on a torn 10½"x6½" piece of vellum. Toddi also shaped the wire into swirls and twirls to echo the patterned papers. Cute dog print buttons anchor the vellum. A picture perfect page!

- **patterned Paper Pizazz™**: light brown swirls, dark brown swirls (*Swirls & Twirls*)
- **vellum Paper Pizazz™**: ivory (available by the sheet)
- **solid Paper Pizazz™**: ivory (*Solid Pastel Papers*)
- **24-gauge copper wire:** Artistic Wire Ltd.
- **dog print buttons:** Dress It Up
- **black pen:** Sakura Gelly Roll
- **designer:** Toddi Barclay

Mini Classes

It's 10:00 on a Saturday night. The house is wonderfully quiet and the kids are finally asleep. You've been busy all week and now you're ready to scrapbook. The only problem? You're stuck for an idea!

The solution! A class! What? At 10:00 on a Saturday night? Why not? Here are 14 fabulous classes you can take whenever you wish. What about a class on creating a rolled frame, distressing paper and embellishments for an aged look or embossing on metal? From Arlene's pin-tucking technique to Susan's big heart pocket, we have a class that will surely jump-start your creativity. Even better, you don't have to leave your house!

Each class includes instructions on the technique plus patterns, if needed. Some of the techniques are new ways to use classic tools, such as the Nested and Diamond Folds templates. Other classes bring you brand-new methods and materials, such as foam board pages and serendipity squares.

Scrapbook teachers and store owners, these mini-classes are terrific for teaching your own classes. Use our designer examples or create your own, based on the techniques.

Are you ready for class? Sharpen your pencils and turn the page to learn the latest in scrapbooking techniques from the Scrapbook Specialists themselves!

Arlene is an avid seamstress in addition to her scrapbooking love. "I decided to combine my favorite activities by pin tucking scrapbook paper," explained Arlene. Cut two 2"x11" or 2"x12" paper strips and glue to form a 22" or 24" length. Then measure ½" and fold under ⅛"; measure ½" and fold under ⅛". Repeat pin tucking the entire length. "Often I've found I need to mat the pin tucking piece so it really is set off from my background paper," offered Arlene. "Once you get going, you'll find it's fast and easy to add a pin tucked embellishment to your page."

1 *fold the top dashed lines toward you*

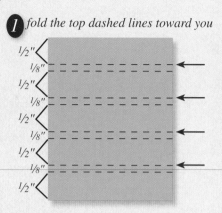

½"
⅛"
½"
⅛"
½"
⅛"
½"
⅛"
½"

2 *fold back along the lower dashed lines to form a pleat*

1 Arlene folded pin tucks along a 2"x22" strip of green vines paper (see her instructions above), matted it on green vellum and glued it to a green sponged paper background.

2 She wrapped fiber around a ¾"x11" green vellum strip. Notice she wrapped it diagonally to set it off from the straight edge of the pin tucking.

3 She matted her photo on green vellum, green vines and again on vellum. She glued fiber along the right and left side of the mat.

4 She computer journaled on green vellum, matted it on green vines and again on vellum. She glued fiber along the right and left side of the mat. Notice the journaling is the same width as the matted photo. With the fibers throughout the page, there is a unified look.

- **patterned Paper Pizazz™:** green vines, green sponge (*Soft & Subtle Textures*)
- **vellum Paper Pizazz™:** pastel green (*Pastel Vellum Papers*, also by the sheet)
- **pastel fibers:** Adornaments™
- **designer:** Arlene Peterson

The world is full of beauty when the heart is full of love.

Alice
June 2002

Arlene combined pin tucks and butterflies to decorate this lovely page. She cut around the lace border along the bottom of the collage paper, matted it on silver; then glued it even with the bottom edge of a 12"x2" strip of blue vellum and glued it back to the bottom of the collage paper. Arlene double pin tucked by using a 1½"x22" strip of vellum vines and a 1¾"x22" strip of silver. She placed the vellum centered on the silver and followed the directions on page 78, except she made four tucks at the top and bottom and four in the middle. She matted Alyshia's photo on silver, vellum vines and blue vellum and attached it to the page with a brad in each corner as shown. She punched silver butterflies and glued them to the pin tuck border and right edge of the photo as shown. She journaled on a 7"x1" strip of blue vellum and attached it below the photo with a brad at each end. She attached the remaining brads as shown.

- **patterned Paper Pizazz™:** white lace collage on blue (*Pretty Collage Papers*)
- **specialty Paper Pizazz™:** vellum vines (*Vellum Papers*, also by the sheet); pastel blue vellum (*Pastel Vellum Papers*, also by the sheet); silver (*Metallic Silver*, also by the sheet)
- **⅛" silver brads:** AmericanPin/Hyglo®
- **⅞", 1⅛" wide butterfly punches:** Marvy® Uchida
- **⅛" hole punch:** Fiskars®
- **designer:** Arlene Peterson

Two columns of pin tucking set the stage for the Peterson's portrait in this memorable page. Arlene matted a 9¾"x10" rectangle of silver on black, leaving a ⅛" border and glued it centered on the stripes paper. She cut two 2¼"x9¾" strips of black and glued one ⅛" from each side of the silver rectangle. Arlene cut four 2"x12" strips from the cross-stitch paper and followed the directions on page 78. She punched silver hearts, wrapped each in floss in random angles and glued to the pin tuck strips. She matted her photo on black and glued it centered between the pin tuck strips. She journaled on a 4½"x2½" silver rectangle, matted it on black and glued it centered below the photo.

- **patterned Paper Pizazz™:** red/black/white stripes, red/black cross-stitch (*Mixing Heritage Papers*)
- **specialty Paper Pizazz™:** silver (*Metallic Silver*, also by the sheet)
- **solid Paper Pizazz™:** black (*Solid Jewel Tones*)
- **1¼" wide heart punch:** Family Treasures, Inc.
- **black/silver embroidery floss:** DMC
- **designer:** Arlene Peterson

To make the frame: Two papers are cut to identical sizes, then glued back-to-back. Using a ruler and X-acto® knife, cut two diagonal lines (making an "X") which end ½"-1" before the paper corners. Then lift each cut and roll (rather than fold) it back. A glue dot, brad or eyelet is strong enough to keep the roll in place. Glue your matted photo to the back of the frame. To keep the frame from flattening, cut a 2"x11" piece of paper, tightly roll it up then glue it under the rolled section, close to the photo.

Option: you can let them extend beyond the frame as Arlene showed with her snowflake frame on the next page, or roll them so they're even with the frame as Lisa did below.

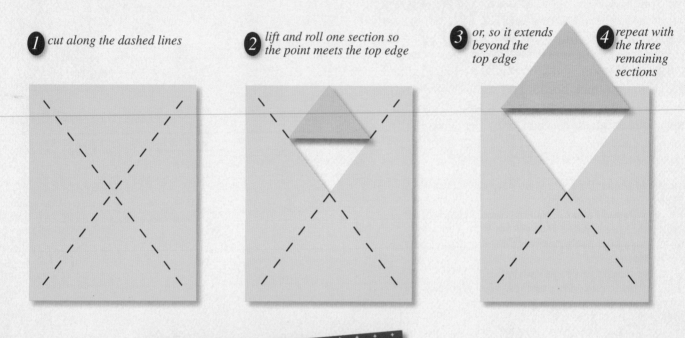

1 cut along the dashed lines

2 lift and roll one section so the point meets the top edge

3 or, so it extends beyond the top edge

4 repeat with the three remaining sections

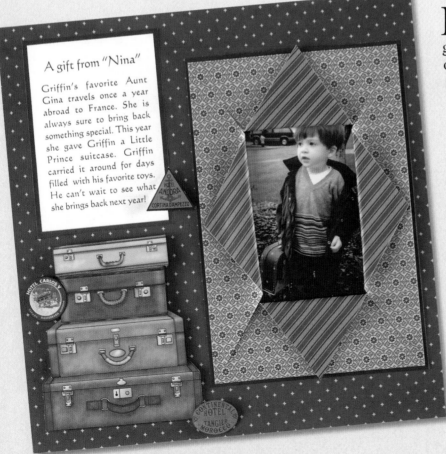

A gift from "Nina"

Griffin's favorite Aunt Gina travels once a year abroad to France. She is always sure to bring back something special. This year she gave Griffin a Little Prince suitcase. Griffin carried it around for days filled with his favorite toys. He can't wait to see what she brings back next year!

Lisa packed a few of her favorite techniques into this fun page. She glued the backs of 5⅞"x8¾" rectangles of green tiles and green stripes, then followed the directions above. She placed a photo behind the window, matted the rectangle on green and glued it to the page. She cut out the *Stack 'ems* suitcases and travel stickers. Lisa used multiple layers of foam tape to attach them to the page as shown. She journaled on white, matted it on green and glued it to the upper left corner of the page. A fun peek at Griffin!

- **patterned Paper Pizazz™**: green stripes, green tiles, twinkling stars on green (*Mixing Heritage Papers*)
- **solid Paper Pizazz™**: green (*Solid Jewel Tones*); white (*Plain Pastel Papers*)
- **Paper Pizazz™ Stack 'em Cut-Outs™**
- **foam adhesive tape:** Therm O Web
- **scrap paper**
- **X-acto® knife, cutting surface:** Hunt Manufacturing Company
- **designer:** Lisa Garcia-Bergstedt

As with each snowflake, Arlene showed each scrapbook page is as unique. She cut a 6½"x8½" vellum snowflake rectangle and followed the directions on page 80 to make the frame. She cropped her photo, matted it on silver, leaving a ½" border, then glued it behind the frame. She matted the frame on blue snowflakes then again on silver, leaving ⅛" borders. Arlene opened the frame and folded the top and bottom sections again toward the center. She supported the rolls with paper. She punched snowflakes from blue snowflakes and vellum snowflakes, layered them and secured each with a brad, then inserted one near the tip of each frame. She tore the right sides of a 2⅞"x12" strip of blue snowflakes and a 3½"x12" strip of white vellum then layered them along the left side of the background paper. She used die-cut letters in silver, glued them on a 1⅞"x11" snowflake vellum and glued the strip centered on the blue snowflake border.

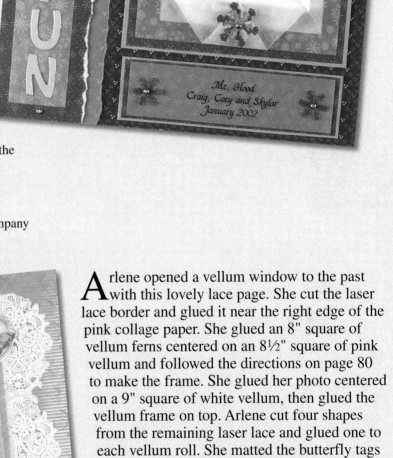
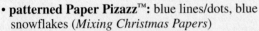

- **patterned Paper Pizazz™:** blue lines/dots, blue snowflakes (*Mixing Christmas Papers*)
- **specialty Paper Pizazz™:** snowflake vellum (*Vellum Papers*, also by the sheet); silver (*Metallic Silver*, also by the sheet); white vellum (by the sheet)
- **⅛" wide silver brads:** AmericanPin/Hyglo®
- **1¼" Traveler letter die-cuts:** Accu/Cut® Systems
- **⅞", 1¼" wide snowflake punches:** Marvy® Uchida
- **X-acto® knife, cutting surface:** Hunt Manufacturing Company
- **designer:** Arlene Peterson

Arlene opened a vellum window to the past with this lovely lace page. She cut the laser lace border and glued it near the right edge of the pink collage paper. She glued an 8" square of vellum ferns centered on an 8½" square of pink vellum and followed the directions on page 80 to make the frame. She glued her photo centered on a 9" square of white vellum, then glued the vellum frame on top. Arlene cut four shapes from the remaining laser lace and glued one to each vellum roll. She matted the butterfly tags onto the solid white paper from the laser lace, both with ⅛" borders, and glued them to the page as shown. A lovely look!

- **patterned Paper Pizazz™:** pink leaf collage (*Pretty Collage Papers*)
- **specialty Paper Pizazz™:** pastel pink vellum (*Pastel Vellum Papers*, also by the sheet); 2 sheets of laser lace (by the sheet); white vellum, vellum ferns (*Vellum Papers*, also by the sheet)
- **butterfly:** *Paper Pizazz™ Tag Art Cut-Outs™*
- **X-acto® knife, cutting surface:** Hunt Mfg. Co.
- **designer:** Arlene Peterson

We first heard about these on the internet. Briefly, they're a large square of plain paper upon which small randomly torn papers are glued, creating a mini work of art. Often the papers are torn allowing a white edge to show—that way each torn piece has its own white mat. Patterned papers, plain papers and vellums are used. Once the large square is covered, it's cut into smaller squares and used to embellish album pages. The squares can be further accented with fibers, eyelets, brads, punched items, buttons and mats—well, you get the idea. The serendipity part is the wonderful way the torn pieces come together. For best results, choose papers which coordinate in a serendipitous way, of course!

1 Lisa matted her photo on white, then mauve and again on white. She used one mauve collage paper for the background.

2 She cut four 2¼"x⅝" strips of white vellum, wrapped one around each corner and glued the ends at the back.

3 Lisa made an 8" serendipity square, using the collage companion paper and mauve. She cut twelve 2" squares and twelve 1" squares and matted each on white. She glued the 2" squares to the page then used foam tape to attach the 1" squares turned on point.

6 She used a black pen to journal above and below the photo.

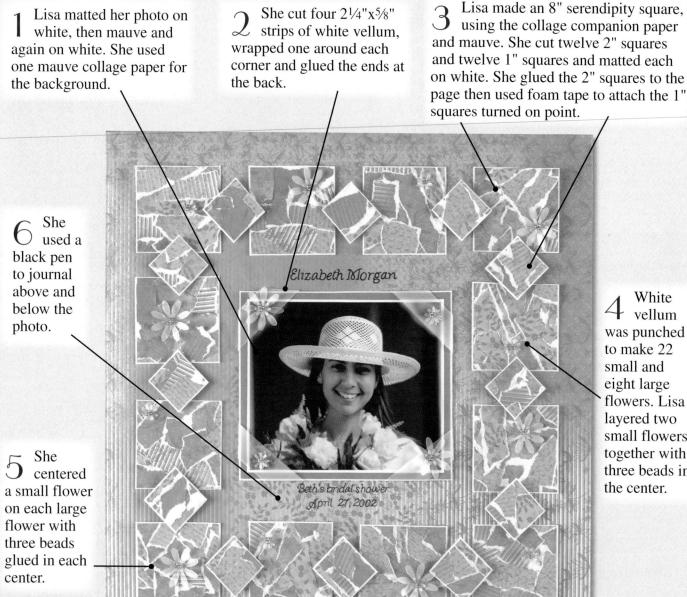

Elizabeth Morgan

Beth's bridal shower
April 27, 2002

4 White vellum was punched to make 22 small and eight large flowers. Lisa layered two small flowers together with three beads in the center.

5 She centered a small flower on each large flower with three beads glued in each center.

- **patterned Paper Pizazz™:** 2 sheets of mauve collage companion papers (*Pretty Collage Papers*)
- **vellum Paper Pizazz™:** white (by the sheet)
- **solid Paper Pizazz™:** mauve (*Solid Muted Colors*); white (*Plain Pastels*)
- **gold seed beads:** Blue Moon Beads/Elizabeth Ward & Co., Inc.
- **⅜" wide flower punch:** Fiskars®
- **1" wide flower punch:** Family Treasures, Inc.
- **white thread, sewing needle**
- **black pen:** Sakura Micron
- **foam adhesive tape:** Therm O Web
- **Keep A Memory ™ Adhesive:** Therm O Web
- **designer:** Lisa Garcia-Bergstedt

Lisa adorned her serendipity squares with textured embellishments for this adorable page. She cropped her photo and matted it on white, lavender sponged, and again on white. The photo was glued at an angle on the splattered paper. She cut a 6"x4½" rectangle of floral and a 6"x6¼" of sponged paper, tearing only along the top edge of each. Lisa matted the layered rectangles on white, leaving a ¹⁄₁₆" border only on the left side. She attached the mat with the eyelets. Lisa made a 6" serendipity white square using the remaining papers. Then she cut one 5⅛"x2¼" rectangle plus five 1½" squares and matted each on white with ¹⁄₁₆" borders. Fibers and buttons embellished the squares as shown. Foam tape attached the squares. Lisa journaled on white, matted it on dark lavender and glued it to the center of the serendipity rectangle.

- **patterned Paper Pizazz™:** lavender floral, lavender splattered, lavender sponged, lavender crystalized (*Soft & Subtle Textures*)
- **solid Paper Pizazz™:** dark lavender (*Solid Jewel Tones*); white (*Plain Pastels*)
- **⅛" dark lavender eyelets:** Stamp Studio
- **purple, lavender fibers:** Adornaments™
- **¾" wide purple, ⅝" wide lavender buttons:** Making Memories
- **foam adhesive tape:** Therm O Web
- **Keep A Memory™ Adhesive:** Therm O Web
- **designer:** Lisa Garcia-Bergstedt

Serendipity squares filled Arlene's imagination to create this lovely page. She cut a 10½"x8½" of purple floral and tore the bottom edge. She matted it on purple and white vellums, each with a torn bottom edge. She matted her photo on white, then purple and again on white. She journaled on a 3⅛"x7" rectangle of white vellum, then matted it on blue vellum, both with top and bottom torn edges. Arlene made a 5¼" serendipity white square using the remaining papers. She cut five 1¾" squares plus two 1" squares and matted each on white with a ⅛" border. She placed each large square on point, glued the second and fourth to the bottom of the page, then used foam tape to attach each end and center square overlapping. She glued fiber across the squares as shown and attached 1" squares to the journal box, with a length of fiber on top.

- **patterned Paper Pizazz™:** brush strokes, purple with white lines, purple floral (*Mixing Light Papers*)
- **vellum Paper Pizazz™:** pastel purple (*Pastel Vellum Papers*, also by the sheet); white (by the sheet)
- **solid Paper Pizazz™:** white (*Plain Pastels*)
- **multi-pastel fibers:** Adornaments™
- **designer:** Arlene Peterson

Although this Nested Shapes template was created for card makers, scrapbookers have captured it for their own. The template offers three nested shape designs, but you can mix them as shown on pages 84-87. Discover the possibilities as you mix and match patterned papers, mat some layers, use vellums, buttons, fibers and beads. If you'd like a metallic edge on a vellum layer, Susan recommends using a gold or silver pen as you trace the template onto your vellum. Then cut out the shape leaving the metallic edge. It's easier than trying to draw a gold line after you've cut the shape. As you'll see, the nested shapes template works for many scrapbook themes and you can choose to use 4-5 as layers or 1-2 as photo corners, borders or page accents. So many choices!

She matted Kaelin's photo on gold, then on red floral and again on gold. She journaled on white and matted it on gold. Shauna inserted an eyelet near each top corner, then threaded ribbon into the eyelets, pulled each end even in the back, crossed them and inserted the ends in the opposite eyelet to the front. She outlined in gold two 3D template shapes from red floral. She used the template to cut out the 1A, 1B, 1C, 1D shapes as shown and matted each on gold, leaving a 1/16" border. She inserted brads and eyelets, then layered the shapes as shown with foam tape and glued the remaining red rose shape centered on top of the ribbon.

- **patterned Paper Pizazz™:** red/gold mesh, gold trees on green stripes, gold/ivory dots, gold stars on green, gold/ivory roses (*Metallic Gold*); gold/red roses, gold (*Metallic Gold*, also by the sheet)
- **solid Paper Pizazz™:** white (*Plain Pastels*)
- **Paper Flair™ Nested Shapes Template**
- **12" of 5/8" green sheer ribbon:** C.M. Offray & Son, Inc.
- **1/2" wide gold stars, 1/2" wide gold heart brads:** AmericanPin/Hyglo®
- **1/8" wide gold eyelets:** Stamp Studio
- **foam adhesive tape:** Therm O Web
- **gold pen:** Sakura Gelly Roll
- **designer:** Shauna Berglund-Immel

Christmas shimmered onto Shauna's page with sparkle and shine. She cut a 9" square of gold trees, matted it on gold and glued it to the mesh paper.

Shauna decorated her favorite hero with patriotic nested shapes and tags in this stunning page. She used the template with the white pen to cut 3A from red/ivory stripes paper. She glued a 5"x7" blue stars rectangle onto the lower left corner, then glued a 12"x5⅛" stars on navy across the top to cover the cut out area. She journaled on ivory, matted it and her heirloom photo on red, then matted the photo on ivory. She cut out the "U", "S" and "A" tags, inserted eyelets, tied a fiber thread through each and used foam tape to attach them to the page. She wrapped a fiber strand of each color across the top of the page, inserted star brads to secure them in front and glued the ends at the page back. She used the template with the white pen to cut out 3A, 3B and 3C, then layered them with foam tape. Shauna inserted the remaining eyelet in the stamp tag, tied the thread and looped it around the cut-out seal placed on top of the nested shapes.

- **patterned Paper Pizazz™**: blue stars on ivory, red/ivory diagonal stripes with stars (*Mixing Heritage Papers*); white stars on navy (by the sheet)
- **solid Paper Pizazz™:** dark red (*Solid Jewel Tones*); ivory (*Plain Pastels*)
- **Paper Pizazz™ *Tag Art Cut-Outs*™:** USA seal, letters, flag stamp tag
- **Paper Flair™ Nested Shapes Template**
- **red, white, blue fibers:** Adornments™
- **metallic gold thread:** DMC
- **½" wide gold star brads:** AmericanPin/Hyglo®
- **⅛" wide gold eyelets:** Stamp Studio
- **foam adhesive tape:** Therm O Web
- **white pen:** Pentel Milky Gel Roller
- **designer:** Shauna Berglund-Immel

Shauna's nested shapes blossomed into a beautiful flower on this lovely page. She tore 1½"-4½" wide strips from the green patterned papers and layered them along the bottom of the blue mini flower paper. She matted her photo on white, then blue paisley and again on white. She tucked the lower corner under a green swirls layer. She cut a ¼"x6" green swirls strip for a stem, matted it on white and inserted the bottom behind the torn strips. She cut two dark green floral/leaves, matted each on white and attached with foam tape. She used the template to cut 2A, 2B, 2C and 2D from the rose patterned papers and matted each on white. Shauna attached six beads in the center of the smallest shape, then layered the shapes with foam tape. She journaled on a white oval, matted it on rose paisley and again on white.

- **patterned Paper Pizazz™:** light green floral, dark green floral, light green sprigs, dark green sprigs, green swirls & dots, light green tiles, rose paisley, rose/pink stripes, pink floral, pink mini floral, blue paisley, blue mini floral (*12"x12" Muted Tints*)
- **solid Paper Pizazz™:** white (*Plain Pastels*)
- **Paper Flair™ Nested Shapes Template**
- **white seed beads:** Blue Moon Beads/Elizabeth Ward & Co., Inc.
- **gold thread, sewing needle**
- **foam adhesive tape:** Therm O Web
- **tracing paper, transfer paper**
- **designer:** Shauna Berglund-Immel

S hauna froze a moment in time with striking snowflakes composed of nested shapes. She used the snowflake collage paper for a stunning background and glued a rhinestone in the center of the three snowflakes in the upper left corner of the page. She matted each photo on silver, then on blue lavender vellum. She glued both photos onto a torn 6½"x10½" white vellum rectangle. Shauna tore a 9½"x2½" rectangle of light blue vellum and glued it between the photos. She used the template and a white pen to cut 3C, 1D, 2D and 3D nested shapes from the vellums. She nested them as shown and glued them at the ends of fiber strands. She glued a rhinestone to the center of each snowflake and at the ends of the blue vellum strip. She used the black pen for journaling.

- **patterned Paper Pizazz**™: snowflake collage (*Vacation Collage Papers*)
- **specialty Paper Pizazz**™: light blue vellum, blue lavender vellum (*Pastel Vellum Papers*); white vellum (by the sheet); silver (*Metallic Silver*, also by the sheet)
- **Paper Flair**™ **Nested Shapes Template**
- **white fibers:** Adornaments™
- **clear round acrylic rhinestones:** Westrim® Crafts
- **glue dots:** Glue Dots™ International LLC
- **black, white pens:** Sakura Gelly Roll
- **designer:** Shauna Berglund-Immel

S hauna garnished her memories of Thanksgiving dinner with nested shapes in this exquisite page. She printed the menu on white and cropped her photo to the same size. She matted each onto gold, then on ivory vellum. She used the gold pen to outline each vellum edge, then inserted an eyelet in the top corners of both. She tore a 12"x1½" strip of vellum and glued it to the top edge of the "give thanks" paper. She glued a fiber strand centered on the vellum strip. Shauna used the template to cut two sets of 3B, 3C and 3D shapes from the fall leaves collage paper and matted each on vellum. She cut four additional 3D shapes from the leaves paper, tracing each with the gold pen. She stacked the two sets of nested shapes, inserted a washer and brad in each center and glued them to the page. She tied thread through the eyelets on the menu and looped it onto the nested shape brad as shown and repeated with the photo set. She inserted a washer and brad in the center of each single shape and glued them along the fiber. She journaled with the black pen.

- **patterned Paper Pizazz**™: give thanks collage, fall leaves collage (*Holidays & Seasons Collage Papers*)
- **specialty Paper Pizazz**™: ivory vellum (*Pastel Vellum Papers*, also by the sheet); gold (*Metallic Gold*, also by the sheet)
- **solid Paper Pizazz**™: white (*Plain Pastels*)
- **Paper Flair**™ **Nested Shapes Template**
- **orange fibers:** Adornaments™

- **gold thread:** Wrights®
- **¼" gold washers, six ³⁄₁₆" gold brads:** AmericanPin/Hyglo®
- **⅛" wide gold eyelets:** Stamp Studio
- **glue dots:** Glue Dots™ International LLC
- **gold, black pens:** Sakura Gelly Roll
- **designer:** Shauna Berglund-Immel

Arlene adorned this delightful page in soft nested shapes for a baby's touch. She cut an 8¼"x11" of blue plaid, tore along the right edge; matted it on white and tore along it's right edge, then glued it to the stars on stripes paper. She matted Tyler's photo on white, then on the blue moons paper and again on white. She journaled on a white rectangle, matted it on blue moons, then on white. She wrapped a 14" length of each fiber and glued the ends at the back. She used the template to cut two 1B, three 3B, three 1D and four 3D nested shapes from the patterned papers as shown and matted each on white. She used foam tape to layer the sets as shown and attach them along the fibers. Arlene tied a yellow fiber through each button and glued them as shown.

- **patterned Paper Pizazz™:** blue plaid, yellow/blue plaid, blue moons/yellow stars, stars on stripes (*Mixing Baby Papers*)
- **solid Paper Pizazz™:** white (*Plain Pastels*)
- **Paper Flair™ Nested Shapes Template**
- **yellow, white, blue fibers:** Adornaments™
- **¾", two ½" white star buttons:** Dress It Up
- **foam adhesive tape:** Therm O Web
- **designer:** Arlene Peterson

Peach dahlias inspired Arlene to create this delightful page. She glued a 9" square of plaid in the lower right corner of the yellow paper, ⅛" above the bottom edge. Then glued a 2½"x9" of peach stripes to the left. She glued a 9"x2½" of peach floral centered above the plaid square and a 2½" peach dots square in the upper left corner. She matted each photo on yellow paper and peach vellum then glued them overlapping. She used the template to cut one 1A, one 3B and two 1D shapes and matted each on vellum. She wrapped each matted 1D shape with fibers. She layered the nested shapes with foam tape and glued buttons to the top piece. She journaled on a vellum rectangle and glued it to the floral rectangle as shown.

- **patterned Paper Pizazz™:** peach plaid, peach flowers on strips, peach floral, peach dots (*Mixing Light Papers*)
- **vellum Paper Pizazz™:** pastel peach (*Pastel Vellum Papers*, also by the sheet)
- **solid Paper Pizazz™:** 2 sheets of pale yellow (*Plain Pastel Papers*)
- **Paper Flair™ Nested Shapes Template**
- **peach fibers:** Adornaments™
- **⁹⁄₁₆" wide peach buttons:** Dress It Up
- **foam adhesive tape:** Therm O Web
- **designer:** Arlene Peterson

Although the *Diamond Folds Template* was developed for cardmakers, scrapbookers have quickly discovered its many wonderful uses. Simply select one of the 14 designs on the template, then place it over your paper or vellum and lightly trace with a pencil. Remove the template, then cut along the traced lines using an X-acto® knife and ruler. Fold the large cuts beginning with the bottom one. (We suggest using a new blade in your X-acto® knife for precise cutting.) Optional: Then add metallic lines along the cut edges. Here are some terrific looks for this versatile template.

8 The last flower was attached to the small tag, then a hole was punched at the top. Fiber was inserted through the hole.

9 She matted her photo on silver and purple vellum, each with an ⅛" border.

7 Susan cut five single flowers, outlined each in silver, then glued tiny marbles to each center. Foam tape was used to attach each flower to the chevrons as shown.

6 Susan chose the lower right design on the template. She traced it onto vellum, made the folds, then outlined the edges with the silver pen. She cut close to the folds and glued the vellum to her tag.

1 Susan glued an 8¾"x11¼" rectangle of checks paper centered on pink flowers on green background. Then she glued a 12"x4" strip of purple vellum across the middle.

2 Two 6"x5" rectangles of purple flowers paper were each matted on silver, leaving a 1/16" border. One is glued near the upper left and the other in the lower right corner. Notice the left paper is placed vertically and the right is placed horizontally.

David & Jen

Our Engagement May 4, 2002

5 She used the template to cut one 1⅛" wide tag and one 2⅝" wide tag from flowers with green leaves. The smaller tag was matted on vellum, then silver; while the larger tag is matted only on silver. She cut a 1½"x4½" window centered on the larger tag and glued vellum to the back, then used the template to cut eight chevrons in the vellum.

4 Susan glued a 7⅝"x5½" rectangle of purple flower vellum, used the silver pen to outline the edge, then glued it at an angle in the page center.

3 Two 5"x6" rectangles of flowers with green leaves paper were each matted on silver, leaving a 1/16" border; then placed overlapping in the center.

- **patterned Paper Pizazz™**: pink flowers on green, lavender/ pink/green checks, lavender flowers with green leaves, large lavender flowers, lavender flowers on pink vellum (*Joy's Soft Collection of Papers*)
- **specialty Paper Pizazz™**: metallic silver (*Metallic Silver*, also by the sheet); pastel purple vellum (*Pastel Vellum Papers*, also by the sheet)

- **Paper Flair™ Templates**: Diamond Folds, Tags
- **tiny glass silver marbles**: Halcraft USA
- **pastel pink fibers**: Magic Scraps
- **¼", ⅛" hole punches**: Marvy® Uchida
- **foam adhesive tape**: Therm O Web
- **silver, pink pens**: Sakura Gelly Roll
- **X-acto® knife, cutting surface**: Hunt Mfg. Co.
- **designer**: Susan Cobb

Natalie is ready for an E... ... ... y page. Paris wrapped t... ... ...e top and bottom edges of t... ...aper, then glued the ends at th... ...er ribbon on top. From wh... ... square and 6¼"x1⅜" s... ...ate to cut the oval. Paris used... ...late to cut the diamond an... ...vellum pieces as shown. She... ...chevrons down, glued each in... ...on the folds. Paris used pi... ...llum pieces to the page. Natalie... ...pink, then trimmed to a ¹⁄₁₆" b... ...left of the diamonds on the v... ...d the black pen to write on the... ...om strip.

- **patterned Paper P**... ...ral (8½"x11" *Collage Papers*)
- **specialty Paper P**... *...ellum Papers*, also by the sheet)
- **solid Paper Pizaz**... ...)
- **Paper Pizazz™ te**... ...lds, Windows #2
- **¼" wide pink sm**... ...es
- **13" of 1½" wid**... ...Offray Designer Ribbons™
- **13" of ⅝" wide pi**... ... Sheer Creations
- **pink glitter, Scappy Glue**™: M... Scraps
- **X-acto® knife, cutting surface:** Hunt Mfg. Co.
- **black pen:** Zig® Writer
- **designer:** Paris Dukes

(See page 126 for the companion page.)

Trimming the tree begins with the cut, so what better theme than diamond cuts for this festive page! Paris used dark green holly patterned paper for the background. She matted her photo on dark green and burgundy papers, each with a ¹⁄₁₆" border, then on green holly, leaving a ¼" border. She glued the matted photo centered on a 7¼"x10½" of green vellum then centered on the right side of the page. She glued a 4½"x1½" of green vellum angled across the corner of the photo mat. Paris cut a 3"x9¼" of green vellum, then used the template to cut five top chevrons and five bottom chevrons centered on the strip. She glued the folded chevrons in place, then used glue dots to attach tiny buttons as shown. She tied floss through the buttons and glued them to the page.

- **patterned Paper Pizazz™:** green holly, dark green holly (*Swirls & Twirls*)
- **specialty Paper Pizazz™:** pastel green vellum (*Pastel Vellum Papers*, also by the sheet)
- **solid Paper Pizazz™:** burgundy, dark green (*New Soft Muted Tints*)
- **Paper Flair™ Diamond Folds Template**
- **⅛" green, ⅛" burgundy, ⁷⁄₁₆" green, ⁷⁄₁₆" burgundy, ¾" green round; ⅝" burgundy heart buttons:** Magic Scraps
- **black embroidery floss:** DMC
- **X-acto® knife, cutting surface:** Hunt Mfg. Co.
- **glue dots:** Glue Dots™ International LLC
- **black pen:** Zebra Jimnie Gel Rollerball
- **designer:** Paris Dukes

Fine leather and heirloom photos are cherished items. Susan combined both in this page. She glued a 10½" tan vellum square centered on a tan leather background, then glued a 1½"x10½" ivory vellum strip down the vellum center. Susan cut two 3" squares of ivory vellum, then cut each in half diagonally. She used the template and knife to cut diamond folds into each triangle. She used the needle and floss to sew one in each corner of the tan vellum square. Susan cut six 2" squares and one 6⅜"x7¾" of filigree, matted each on brown, then black, with 1/16" borders. She glued two squares to each side, then centered the large square on the page. She sewed a button to each remaining square, then glued them as shown. She matted her photo on ivory and tan vellums, each with a ⅛" border, then placed it on the page with photo corners. She used the ribbon to make a showstring bow and glued it above the left photo corner. She used the brown pen for journaling.

- **patterned Paper Pizazz™**: tan "leather", tan embossed filigree ("Leather" Papers)
- **specialty Paper Pizazz™**: 2 sheets of tan vellum (Pastel Vellum Papers, also by the sheet); ivory vellum (by the sheet)
- **solid Paper Pizazz™**: brown (Solid Muted Colors); black (Solid Jewel Tones)
- **Paper Flair™ Diamond Folds Template**
- **7/16" wide black buttons:** Magic Scraps
- **metallic copper embroidery floss:** DMC
- **10" of 5/8" wide black sheer ribbon:** C.M. Offray & Son, Inc.
- **black photo corners:** Canson-Talens, Inc.
- **brown pen:** Sakura Pigma Micron
- **X-acto® knife, cutting surface:** Hunt Manufacturing Company
- **sewing needle**
- **designer:** Susan Cobb

It's a silver anniversary with this elegant theme. Susan used black stripes for a background, then glued a 10¼" silver square in the center. She cut 6" squares of light gray tiles and gray plaid, then cut each diagonally in half. Susan matted each triangle on mauve, leaving a ⅛" border. She overlapped the triangles onto the silver square, so one end tucked under the next. She cut a 2½" dark gray tiles square, cut it diagonally in half, then glued one to the upper right and lower left corners as shown. Susan cut a 7" square of peach vellum, then used the template and knife to cut diamond folds along each side. She used the silver pen to outline the edge and folds, then turned it on point and glued it centered on the page. She matted a 5" dark gray tiles square on silver, leaving a 1/16" border and glued it to the page. She matted her photo on black and used the black pen for journaling. So classic!

- **patterned Paper Pizazz™**: black stripes, dark gray tiles, light gray tiles, gray plaid (Mixing Masculine Papers)
- **specialty Paper Pizazz™**: peach vellum (Pastel Vellum Papers, also by the sheet); 2 sheets of metallic silver (Metallic Silver, also by the sheet)
- **solid Paper Pizazz™**: 2 sheets of mauve (Solid Muted Colors); black (Solid Jewel Tones)
- **Paper Flair™ Diamond Folds Template**
- **silver pen:** Sakura Gelly Roll
- **black pen:** Zig® Writer
- **X-acto® knife, cutting surface:** Hunt Mfg. Co.
- **designer:** Susan Cobb

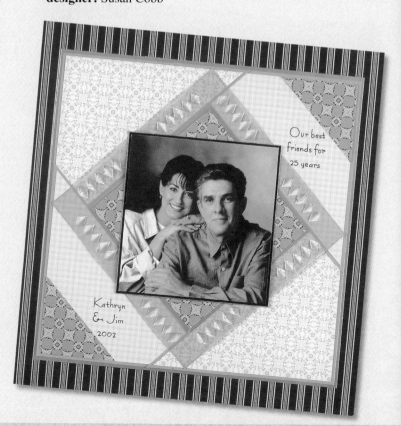

Diamond folds add unexpected dimension to this subtle collage of textures and hues of blue. Susan placed the blue vines paper on a cutting surface and used the knife to cut along each side of the vines column beginning 2½" below the top edge. Susan cut an 8"x12" of white vellum, a 5½"x12" of blue/lavender vellum and a 3½"x12" of dark blue vellum, then tore the long edges of each. Susan lifted the cut vines column, then layered the vellums as shown. She glued a 12"x¼" silver strip across the center, then glued the column in place. Susan tore 2"x9¼" and 3½"x1¼" rectangles of blue/lavender vellum. She used the template to cut two rows of diamond folds as shown, then placed the vellum on the vines and used the silver pen to trace some sprigs. She glued ¼"x3¾" white vellum behind each diamond fold row, then glued the vellum piece centered on the vines column. She journaled on the small vellum piece and glued it near the upper right corner. She matted the photo on silver, then blue vellum, each with a ⅛" border.

- **patterned Paper Pizazz™:** blue vines collage (*Jacie's Collage Papers*)
- **specialty Paper Pizazz™:** blue/lavender vellum, dark blue vellum (*Pastel Vellum Papers*); white vellum (by the sheet); metallic silver (*Metallic Silver*, also by the sheet)
- **Paper Flair™ Diamond Folds Template**
- **silver pen:** Sakura Gelly Roll
- **X-acto® knife, cutting surface:** Hunt Mfg. Co.
- **designer:** Susan Cobb

Susan enhanced the vintage patterned papers with tiny diamond folds cut into vellum for this delightful page. She started with stripes for a background, then glued a 10⅜"x11¼" of mauve flowers even with the bottom edge. She matted a 7½"x11" of "embossed" vines onto silver, leaving a ⅛" border. She cut two 1¼" squares of flowers, cut each diagonally in half, then matted the long edges on vellum. One triangle was glued to each floral rectangle corner, then the piece was glued centered along the page bottom edge. Susan matted the photo on white and lavender papers, then on lavender vellum. For the envelope, Susan cut a 6¼"x4⅝" floral rectangle, scored ¼" from the left and right edges, then across the center. She folded the sides inward, then along the center to form a pocket. She transferred the flap (see page 143) and heart diamond folds patterns onto vellum, then used the knife to cut them out. She used the silver pen to detail the cuts and edges. After folding the cuts, Susan tied a shoestring bow, then glued it to the page as shown.

- **patterned Paper Pizazz™:** mauve flowers & butterflies, mauve/cream stripes, cream vines (*Joy's Vintage Papers*)
- **specialty Paper Pizazz™:** pink-lavender vellum (*Pastel Vellum Papers*); metallic silver (*Metallic Silver*, also by the sheet)
- **solid Paper Pizazz™:** lavender, white (*Plain Pastels*)
- **Paper Flair™ Diamond Folds Template**
- **12" of ⅝" wide dark lavender sheer ribbon:** MSI
- **mauve pen:** Zig® Writer
- **silver pen:** Sakura Gelly Roll
- **X-acto® knife, cutting surface:** Hunt Mfg. Co.
- **designer:** Susan Cobb

Mini envelopes are an easy way to add extra dimension to your pages. With these new templates, you have a variety of shapes and sizes at your fingertips. Often vellum is used for envelopes but try patterned papers or metallic papers to vary the look. Simply trace the envelope onto your paper and cut out (on vellum, be sure to cut off pen or pencil lines). Fold in both sides and then the bottom. You may want to leave the top flap unfolded. See the following pages for ideas. It's so easy!

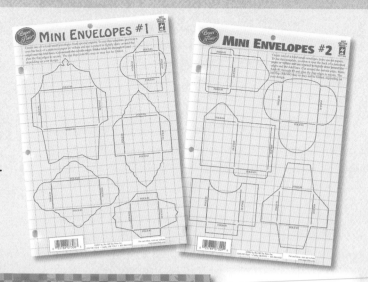

7 Arlene balanced the page top with an eyelet inserted in each top corner of the floral rectangle. She thread fibers through the eyelets then glued the ends at the back.

1 Arlene began this joyful page with a yellow/rose checks background.

2 She matted a 10¼" square of pink dots on yellow onto black, then onto vellum, tearing the vellum edges for a border.

6 Arlene used the pen to journal on the vellum mat below the photo.

3 Arlene matted Alyshia's photo on black and glued it centered near the top of a 6½"x6" torn vellum rectangle. She glued the matted photo centered on a 8¼"x7⅝" rectangle of floral, matted on black.

5 She cut out the "J", "O" and "Y" tags, inserted an eyelet in each and tied fibers through each eyelet. Each tag was inserted into an envelope.

4 Arlene used the template to cut three envelopes from tan vellum. She glued the sides then the bottoms of each envelope, leaving the top flaps open. She wrote on each bottom flap then glued the envelopes evenly spaced below the photo mat.

- **patterned Paper Pizazz**™: yellow/rose checks, pink dots on yellow, yellow flowers on pink (*Mixing Bright Papers*)
- **vellum Paper Pizazz**™: 2 sheets of tan (*Pastel Vellum Papers*, also by the sheet)
- **solid Paper Pizazz**™: black (*Solid Jewel Tones*)

- **Paper Pizazz**™ Tag Art Cut-Outs™
- **Paper Flair**™ Mini Envelopes #1 Template
- **⅛" wide gold eyelets**: Stamp Studio
- **pink, dark green, goldenrod fibers**: Adornments™
- **black pen**: Sakura Gelly Roll
- **designer**: Arlene Peterson

Shauna created a celestial wonderland to remember a special evening with this dazzling page. She matted her photo on gold, the sun collage paper with stars covering the bottom third, again on gold, then on blue vellum. She outlined the vellum edges with the gold pen. She tore a 2"-3" wide vellum strip and attached it with eyelets. She used foam tape to attach the cut-out sun face onto a 1¾" torn square of stars. She cut a tag from remnants of the collage paper, outlined in gold, then inserted one large eyelet. Shauna inserted eyelets on the moon square and glued a star charm as shown. She tied thread through each bottom eyelet and attach each to a tag. She cut the ribbon in half, wrapped one length around each thread and knotted it. She used the template to make two vellum envelopes, outlining each in gold. She inserted a charm, glitter and punched gold stars into each, sealed them then glued one to each tag.

- **patterned Paper Pizazz™:** blue moon metallic collage, blue sun metallic collage (*Metallic Collage Papers*)
- **specialty Paper Pizazz™:** pastel blue vellum (*Pastel Vellum Paper*s, also by the sheet); gold (*Metallic Gold*, also by the sheet)
- **Paper Flair™ Mini Envelopes #1 Template**
- **3/16", two 1/8" wide gold eyelets:** Stamp Studio
- **1" gold moon, 5/8" wide gold star charms:** S. Axelrod Company
- **10" of 1/2" metallic gold ribbon:** Horizon Fabrics, Inc.
- **gold glitter:** Chunky Sparklerz
- **gold thread:** Wrights®
- **1/4" wide star punch:** McGill, Inc.
- **glue dots:** Glue Dots™ International LLC
- **foam adhesive tape:** Therm O Web
- **gold pen:** Sakura Gelly Roll
- **designer:** Shauna Berglund-Immel

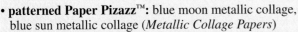

Lisa captured the essence of a precious moment in this stunning page. She began with a sheet of yellow vellum over yellow roses paper. She matted four 6"x1¼" strips of gold/red roses onto gold, then wrapped one around each corner. She cut an 8" square of gold/red roses, turned it on point and used the knife to cut a 3⅜"x2¼" rectangle near the bottom. Then she matted it on gold. Lisa matted Lauren's photo on burgundy and gold. She cut out the vellum envelope, inserted an eyelet into the flap tip. She used the gold pen to outline the top flap with dots along the edge. She wrapped gold thread around her hand ten times, cut the strands, inserted them through the eyelet, pulled the ends even and knotted them together to form a tassle. Lisa cut an inverted "V" into each end an 8"x¾" strip of vellum and used the black pen for journaling.

- **patterned Paper Pizazz™:** gold/red roses, gold (*Metallic Gold*, also by the sheet); yellow roses (by the sheet)
- **vellum Paper Pizazz™:** 2 sheets of pastel yellow (*Pastel Vellum Papers*, also by the sheet)
- **solid Paper Pizazz™:** burgundy (*Solid Jewel Tones*)
- **Paper Flair™ Mini Envelopes #1 Template**
- **3/16" wide gold eyelet:** Stamp Studio
- **gold thread:** DMC
- **gold, black pens:** Sakura Gelly Roll
- **X-acto® knife, cutting surface:** Hunt Mfg. Co.
- **designer:** Lisa Garcia-Bergstedt

An adorable photo inspired Lisa to fashion this playful page. She cut ³⁄₈" wide strips of blue vellum with an inverted "V" cut into the right ends, then outlined each strip with the silver pen. She glued the strips evenly spaced along the left edge of the striped paper. She cut the heart shape from red and outlined it with the silver pen. She matted the heart on vellum, then used foam tape to attach the silver matted photo. She used the template to cut three vellum envelopes and outlined the front flap in silver. She punched six hearts and the letters from red and outlined each letter and three hearts in silver. She used foam tape to attach them. Lisa glued one of the remaining hearts to the flap of each envelope, then inserted an eyelet into the center of each heart. She wrote a descriptive word on three 2⁷⁄₁₆"x1³⁄₈" white rectangles, matted on each on red and inserted one into each envelope. She wrapped two envelopes in thread and glued them to the top and bottom vellum strips. She glued the third envelope open on the center vellum strip, with a strand of thread inserted through the eyelet.

- **patterned Paper Pizazz™**: blue stripes (*Muted Tints*)
- **specialty Paper Pizazz™**: blue vellum (*Pastel Vellum Papers*, also by the sheet), silver (*Metallic Silver*, also by the sheet)
- **solid Paper Pizazz™**: red (*Solid Jewel Tones*); white (*Plain Pastels*)
- **Paper Flair™ Mini Envelopes #1 Template**
- **¹⁄₈" wide red eyelets**: Stamp Studio
- **silver thread**: Wrights®
- **1¼" Traveler letter die-cuts**: Accu/Cut® Systems
- **⁵⁄₈" wide heart punch**: Marvy® Uchida
- **foam adhesive tape**: Therm O Web
- **silver, black pens**: Sakura Gelly Roll
- **tracing paper, transfer paper**
- **designer**: Lisa Garcia-Bergstedt

Shauna lavished her imagination with beads and a vellum envelope to make this fairy wonderland. She trimmed the yellow swirls paper to 8¼"x10¾" and matted it on white. She used the photo tinting pens to enhance a black and white photo, matted it on yellow and white. She punched out the center of the fairies' frame and covered the back of the circle with white vellum. She glued a seed bead to each flower center on the frame, then used foam tape to attach it to the page. She inserted four eyelets as shown. Shauna strung pairs of each color seed beads with alpha beads evenly spaced. She hung them between the two top eyelets, gluing the ends at the back. She cut and folded a yellow vellum envelope, then strung beads from each top corner to an eyelet. She punched a flower from white, glued a seed bead in the center and glued the flower to the front flap. She journaled on white and inserted into the frame.

- **patterned Paper Pizazz™**: yellow swirls (*Bright Tints*, also by the sheet)
- **vellum Paper Pizazz™**: pastel yellow (*Pastel Vellum Papers*, also by the sheet); white (by the sheet)
- **solid Paper Pizazz™**: yellow, white (*Plain Pastels*)
- **Paper Flair™ Mini Envelopes #1 Template**
- *Paper Pizazz™ Girl Power Punch-Outs™*: fairies' frame
- **orange, yellow, white seed beads**: Blue Moon Beads/Elizabeth Ward & Co., Inc.
- **¼" alpha beads**: Darice, Inc.
- **¹⁄₈" wide white eyelets**: Stamp Studio
- **gold thread**: Wrights®
- **³⁄₈" wide flower punch**: Fiskars®
- **foam adhesive tape**: Therm O Web
- **peach, honeycomb, blush photo tinting pens**: Zig® Photo Twin™
- **peach, brown, blush decorating chalks**: Craf-T Products
- **black, white pens**: Sakura Gelly Roll
- **designer**: Shauna Berglund-Immel

Arlene cut two 1" wide strips of butterflies paper then cut one long edge of each with scallop scissors. She matted each strip on blue vellum. She used the letter template to cut "MEMORIES" from check paper and matted each letter on vellum. She arranged the butterfly borders and the letters—mounted with foam tape—at the top of the swirl background. Arlene triple-matted the photo on vellum, check paper and vellum again. She placed it at an angle to add interest. She used the small envelope template to form the envelope from check paper. She placed a 2½"x2¾" vellum rectangle at an angle with the envelope on top. She computer journaled on blue vellum then cut it into a tag using the template. She placed a ⅛" smaller tag from check paper underneath. She cut several different size butterflies from the butterfly paper and mounted them to the page with foam tape.

- **patterned Paper Pizazz™:** blue swirl, blue check, purple butterflies (*Joy's Soft Collection of Papers*)
- **vellum Paper Pizazz™:** pastel blue vellum (*Pastel Vellum Papers,* also by the sheet)
- **templates:** Paper Flair™ 2 Envelopes, Tags
- **"Classic Caps" letters template:** Francis Meyer, Inc.®
- **wide scallop decorative scissors:** Fiskars®
- **foam adhesive tape:** Therm O Web
- **designer:** Arlene Peterson

Natural papers go hand-in-hand with the great outdoors! Arlene cut a 3" wide strip of dark pinecone paper and tore both edges. She matted it on white vellum and stitched them together with jute string. She triple-matted the photo on vellum, dark pinecone with torn edges and vellum again. She stitched them together then tied two tan and one green button on each side. She folded two white vellum envelopes using the template then cut two tags from dark pinecone using the template. Arlene matted the tags on white vellum then inserted an eyelet in each. She threaded jute through the eyelets, continuing the design element. She computer journaled on white vellum then tore the edges. She added two buttons threaded with jute to the journaling.

- **patterned Paper Pizazz™:** dark green pinecone, light green pinecone (*Jacie's Watercolor Naturals*)
- **vellum Paper Pizazz™:** white vellum (by the sheet)
- **Paper Flair™ Tags Template**
- **jute strings:** Dritz
- **brown, green buttons:** Dress It Up
- **⅛" tan eyelets:** Stamp Studio
- **designer:** Arlene Peterson

Susan's big heart pockets make a spectacular addition to scrapbook pages! They're beautiful and versatile—they're also easy to make. The patterns for the pocket and heart insert are on page 143. Cut out each pattern, fold it along each dashed line then unfold it. Place the pocket on the table and press each side inward as you bring the bottom piece upward for a perfect pocket. Use a soft colored vellum for the pocket and patterned paper for the heart, like the one below. Or, do the reverse and create the pocket from patterned paper, as Susan did on page 96. You'll find no matter which paper you choose, your pocket will look stunning!

heart pocket
back or front
(your choice)

9 The photo was matted on metallic gold and glued to the page inside the frame. The ribbon makes a pretty bow on the heart.

8 Susan formed an ivory vellum heart pocket and the heart insert from tan floral on yellow paper. She used the gold pen to outline each, then glued an individual bouquet to the vellum pocket and a butterfly to the heart.

1 Susan began with a large gingham background paper.

2 She cut an 8½"x10½" rectangle of floral paper. Susan used the knife to cut a 4½"x6½" window in the center for a frame.

3 A 6"x8" rectangle of tan floral on yellow was glued to the back of the frame, then a 4"x6" window was cut in the center. Susan used foam tape to attach the frame to the page then snipped the inner tan floral corners and pressed the edges into the foam for a beveled effect.

7 Susan used strips of foam tape to adhere the frame centered on the page.

6 A ⅝" wide strip of pink vellum was glued to trim the outer frame edge between each corner.

5 Each vellum triangle was trimmed with a ³⁄₁₆" wide strip of gold.

4 Susan cut two 3" squares of ivory vellum, then cut each diagonally in half and glued one to each frame corner.

- **patterned Paper Pizazz™:** yellow flowers, green/ivory large gingham, tan floral on yellow (*Joy's Vintage Papers*)
- **specialty Paper Pizazz™:** pastel pink vellum (*Pastel Vellum Papers*, also by the sheet); 2 sheets of ivory vellum (by the sheet); metallic gold (*Metallic Gold*, also by the sheet)
- **12" of ⅝" wide lavender sheer ribbon:** Offray Designs™
- **foam adhesive tape:** Therm O Web
- **gold pen:** Sakura Gelly Roll
- **X-acto® knife, cutting surface:** Hunt Mfg. Co.
- **designer:** Susan Cobb

S hauna's fairytale day is the perfect theme for a heart pocket. Susan began with a purple "leather" background, then glued an 11"x2¾" strip of flower/dots paper at an angle, 2¾" from the upper right corner, then trimmed the ends even with the page. She matted a 7" white vellum square onto an 8" purple vellum square, turned it on point and glued the right half to the page, as shown. She cut a 10"x12" piece of floral embossed paper, placed it as shown and cut out the triangle shape. She trimmed the point with ¼" wide strips of silver. She used the template and knife to cut a 4"x5½" window, then pulled the left point of the vellum diamond through the window. She matted the photo on silver. Susan formed a heart pocket (see page 143) from flowers/dots paper, cut a heart window in the center and glued purple vellum behind it. The insert heart was cut from white vellum. She attached the pearls and bow as shown. Susan used the silver pen to outline the pieces and for journaling.

- **patterned Paper Pizazz™:** purple floral embossed, purple flowers/dots embossed, purple leather (*"Leather" Papers*)
- **specialty Paper Pizazz™:** pastel purple vellum (*Pastel Vellum Papers*, also by the sheet); white vellum (by the sheet); metallic silver (*Metallic Silver*, also by the sheet)
- **Paper Pizazz™ Windows #2 Template**
- **white fused pearls:** Magic Scraps
- **1" wide lavender satin ribbon bow with pearl:** Jesse James
- **⅛" wide hole punch:** Marvy® Uchida
- **silver pen:** Sakura Gelly Roll
- **X-acto® knife, cutting surface:** Hunt Mfg. Co.
- **designer:** Susan Cobb

B ig hearts adorn this lovely page filled with soft vellums and florals. Susan glued a 2"x12" of tiny blue flowers centered on a 4⅝"x12" of light blue vellum. She glued it 2¼" from the left edge of the blue dots background paper. Susan created a geometric photo mat on a 10½"x8¼" blue-lavender vellum piece by gluing a 4½"x7¾" of tiny flowers near the left edge and a 2"x8¼" of floral vellum overlapping the center top right edge. Then, she centered a 7¾"x4½" tiny flowers matted on light blue vellum onto the piece and glued a 1" wide silver strip across the page center. She rolled 1" wide silver strips to form 3", 2¼" and ¾" long rolls, placed foam tape inside each and layered them to form a bow on the silver strip as shown. She matted the photo on silver and blue-lavender vellum and glued it to the right of the bow. She traced the heart pocket and heart shape patterns (see page 143) onto floral and light blue vellums, outlined the edges with the silver pen and glued them as shown. She cut a ⁵⁄₁₆"x2" silver strip, trimmed the corners of each end, folded it in half and glued it to the heart pocket as shown.

- **patterned Paper Pizazz™:** blue dots, tiny blue flowers, blue floral vellum (*Joy's Garden*)
- **specialty Paper Pizazz™:** blue-lavender vellum (*Pastel Vellum Papers*); pastel blue vellum (*Pastel Vellum Papers*, also by the sheet); metallic silver (*Metallic Silver*, also by the sheet)
- **foam adhesive tape:** Therm O Web
- **silver pen:** Sakura Gelly Roll
- **designer:** Susan Cobb

Triangles make amazing looks on scrapbook pages, especially when one triangle is vellum. An easy way to make a traingle is to start with a square or rectangle, then mark the center of one edge and cut from that center mark to the both opposite corners—see, it's easy! Or for a right triangle, begin with a square, fold it diagonally and cut along the fold. Now you have two equal triangles.

Isosceles Triangle

Right Triangle

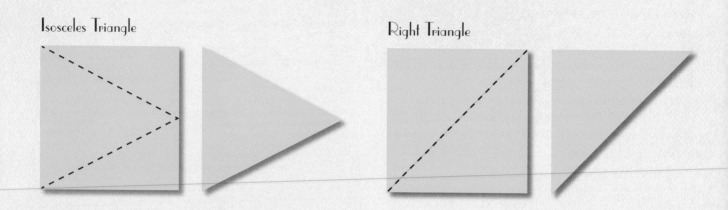

Arlene sculpted a spectacular effect using triangles and patterned papers. She glued a 2¼"x12" rectangle of black ½" from the left edge of the diamonds paper. She cut 1"x11¾" strips of both the solid green and floral papers and glued them as shown. She cut 3⁷⁄₁₆"x7" rectangles of both green and floral papers and glued them to a 7⅛" black square. She cut a 7" square of the floral, measured 3½" down the right side, then cut from the center to the upper and bottom corners on the left to form a triangle. She repeated for a green vellum triangle. She matted the floral on black and glued it pointing to the right, then glued the vellum triangle pointing to the left. She matted her photo on black and glued it centered on the square. She used the pattern to cut six vellum triangles, then used those to make six floral triangles, matting each floral triangle on black. She glued the floral triangles along the left side of the border rectangle, then overlapped the green vellum triangles on top. She inserted a heart brad in the center of the top and bottom triangles. She journaled on a green vellum rectangle, matted it on floral and black papers and inserted a heart at each end.

- **patterned Paper Pizazz**™: green/purple floral, green diamonds (*Coordinating Florals & Patterns*)
- **vellum Paper Pizazz**™: pastel green (*Pastel Vellum Papers*, also by the sheet)
- **solid Paper Pizazz**™: green, black (*Solid Jewel Tones*)
- ⅜" **wide gold heart brads:** AmericanPin/Hyglo®
- **designer:** Arlene Peterson

Lisa layered vellum triangles for this sophisticated page. She cut 10" squares from pink and white vellums, then cut each in half diagonally. She used the gold pen to outline the cut edges and the pattern to draw flowers along the top of one pink and white triangle. She glued the white vellum triangle even with the lower right corner of a lavender collage paper and a pink triangle in the lower left. Lisa matted her photo on gold, then onto the companion collage paper. She outlined the edge in gold and glued it to the page. She placed the remaining pink triangle ¾" below the cut edge of the white triangle and trimed the bottom edge even with the page. She repeated the process with the white triangle then glued both in place. She used the gold pen to journal on the triangles and draw two more flowers.

- **patterned Paper Pizazz™:** lavender collage, lavender collage companion (*Pretty Collage Papers*)
- **specialty Paper Pizazz™:** pastel pink vellum (*Pastel Vellum Paper*s, also by the sheet); white vellum (by the sheet); gold (*Metallic Gold*, also by the sheet)
- **gold pen:** Sakura Gelly Roll
- **designer:** Lisa Garcia-Bergstedt

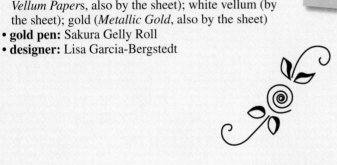

This pretty purple page packs a punch of playfulness! Arlene used big triangles for the background. She marked 6" down the right side of the center of each vellum and lavender butterflies sheet. She cut from each left corner to the mark. She overlapped the triangles with the vellum on top then cut two 7½"x1" strips of gold paper. She tucked one on each side of the vellum triangle and under the lavender one. Arlene used the cut-out butterfly tags and matted them on gold. She punched holes in the two small tags then threaded fibers. She cut three 13" lengths of fibers and placed them on the right side of the page then attached the tags on top with foam tape. Arlene computer journaled on vellum, tore the edges then glued them to the tags. She matted the photo on gold and vellum with three fiber strands wrapped on the left side. She completed the page with gold penwork on the vellum mat and triangle then gold beads on the butterfly wings.

- **patterned Paper Pizazz™:** light lavender butterflies, lavender butterflies (*Jacie's Watercolor Naturals*)
- **specialty Paper Pizazz™:** pastel purple vellum (*Pastel Vellum Papers,* also by the sheet), metallic gold (*Metallic Gold,* also by the sheet)
- **tags:** Paper Pizazz™ Tag Art #2 Cut-Outs™
- **purple fibers:** Adornments™
- **tiny gold beads:** Halcraft USA
- **adhesive foam tape:** Therm O Web
- **gold pen:** Sakura Gelly Roll
- **designer:** Arlene Peterson

If you love the lumpy look in scrapbooking or simply want to add lumpy materials but don't want them pressing into other pages—here's the answer! Foam core boards are found in the art material department of your craft store. They're made of a sheet of foam with paper on each side. You can cut windows into them using an X-acto® knife with a fresh blade. Place the foam board on a cutting surface (bread board, glass or cardboard) and use a knife for straight windows. A template will help you draw straight windows. After making your page (be sure to back the windows with paper), just slip them into a sheet protector and into your album.

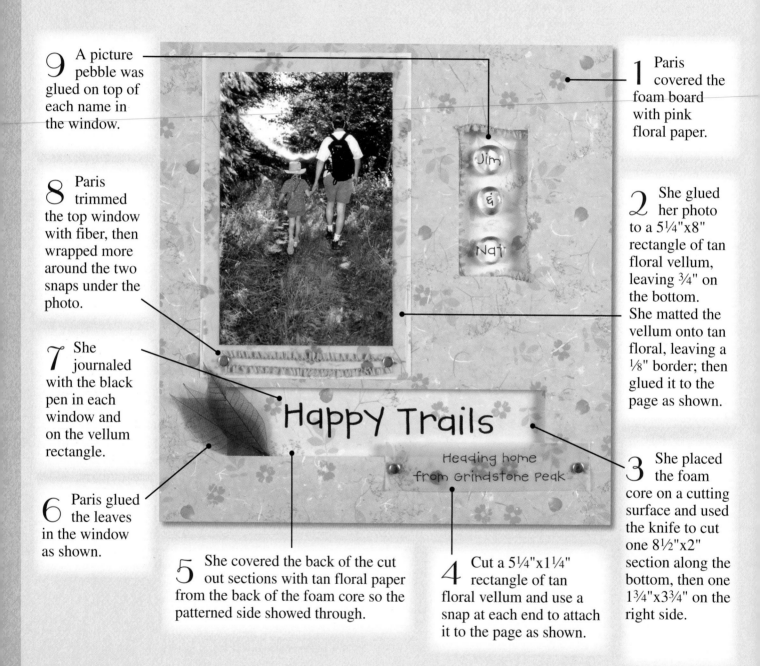

9 A picture pebble was glued on top of each name in the window.

8 Paris trimmed the top window with fiber, then wrapped more around the two snaps under the photo.

7 She journaled with the black pen in each window and on the vellum rectangle.

6 Paris glued the leaves in the window as shown.

5 She covered the back of the cut out sections with tan floral paper from the back of the foam core so the patterned side showed through.

4 Cut a 5¼"x1¼" rectangle of tan floral vellum and use a snap at each end to attach it to the page as shown.

1 Paris covered the foam board with pink floral paper.

2 She glued her photo to a 5¼"x8" rectangle of tan floral vellum, leaving ¾" on the bottom. She matted the vellum onto tan floral, leaving a ⅛" border; then glued it to the page as shown.

3 She placed the foam core on a cutting surface and used the knife to cut one 8½"x2" section along the bottom, then one 1¾"x3¾" on the right side.

Happy Trails

Heading home from Grindstone Peak

- **patterned Paper Pizazz**™: pink floral, tan floral, tan floral vellum (*Flowered "Handmade" Papers*)
- **12" square of white foam core board:** Hunt Mfg. Co.
- **¼" wide silver snaps:** Making Memories
- **clear picture pebbles:** Magic Scraps

- **tan fibers:** Adornaments™
- **dark green skeleton leaves:** Decorative Accents
- **X-acto® knife, cutting surface:** Hunt Manufacturing Co.
- **black pen:** Zig® Writer
- **designer:** Paris Dukes

Treasures for now and forever were selected by Lisa in this spectacular page. She tore the collage paper along the color change, chalked the torn edges, then glued the papers to the foam. Lisa cut out three 3½"x2¼" rectangles, ½" apart on the left side; then cut out around the flower rectangle in the lower right corner. She glued the flower rectangle on ivory and glued it to the foam back with the flower centered in the window. She used the ivory paper to cover the backs of the windows, then tore tan vellum rectangles, crumpled and uncrumpled them, chalked the edges and glued them to cover the inside of the rectangles with portions extending over the sides. She matted her photo on peach, then vellum. She cut three envelopes out of tan paper and folded the sides then the bottom of each. She punched six circles from peach. She placed a circle on each envelope flap, then inserted an eyelet in each. She attached an eyelet in each remaining circle, glued one to each envelope ⅛" below the closed flap, inserted a message and used cording to secure each envelope. She placed an envelope into each window and covered each along the bottom with a 4½"x¾" strip of vellum. She journaled on a torn-edge vellum rectangle and glued it as shown.

- **patterned Paper Pizazz™:** tan letters/flower collage (*Soft Collage Papers*)
- **vellum Paper Pizazz™:** 2 sheets of tan (*Pastel Vellum Papers*, also by the sheet)
- **solid Paper Pizazz™:** peach, tan, ivory (*Plain Pastels*)
- **11½"x12" white foam core board:** Hunt Mfg. Co.
- **⅛" wide gold eyelets:** Stamp Studio
- **brown decorating chalk:** Craf-T Products
- **gold cording**
- **½" wide hole punch:** Fiskars®
- **X-acto® knife, cutting surface:** Hunt Manufacturing Co.
- **black pen:** Sakura Gelly Roll
- **tracing paper, transfer paper**
- **designer:** Lisa Garcia-Bergstedt

Lisa made room for baby and all her special qualities in this delightful page. She covered the foam core with the floral paper, then cut a 5½"x6½" rectangle centered on the page, three 1½" squares on each side and a 5½"x1" rectangle centered below the large opening. She covered the backs of the squares with pink gingham and used the lavender sponged to cover the center rectangles. She twisted the ribbon to thread the alpha beads onto it knotting it after each name and at each end, then glued the beads into the lower center rectangle and wrapped the ribbon ends to the back. She punched each shape from white, chalked each and used foam tape to attach one in each square window. She cut six 2¼"x⁷⁄₁₆" strips of white vellum, journaled on each and inserted an eyelet at each end to secure. She matted her photo on white and glued it inside the large rectangle. She cut a 5⅞"x7¼" of vellum, then a 2¾" window centered near the top. Lisa outlined it in white, journaled with the black pen, then inserted an eyelet in each corner to secure it to the page as shown.

- **patterned Paper Pizazz™:** petite floral, pink gingham, lavender sponged (*Mixing Baby Papers*)
- **vellum Paper Pizazz™:** white (by the sheet)
- **solid Paper Pizazz™:** white (*Plain Pastels*)
- **12" square of white foam core board:** Hunt Mfg. Co.
- **⅛" wide pink eyelets:** Stamp Studio
- **¼" alpha beads:** Darice, Inc.
- **18" of ⅝" wide pink sheer ribbon:** C.M. Offray & Son, Inc.
- **pink, green, blue, yellow, orange decorating chalks:** Craf-T Products
- **½" wide foot, hand punches:** McGill
- **½" wide heart, smile punches:** Marvy® Uchida
- **½" wide flower, moon punches:** Family Treasures, Inc.
- **X-acto® knife, cutting surface:** Hunt Manufacturing Company
- **foam adhesive tape:** Therm O Web
- **white pen:** Sakura Gelly Roll
- **designer:** Lisa Garcia-Bergstedt

Gathered shells and sand provided a rush of ideas for this lovely scene. Lisa glued the palm tree collage paper to the foam core, then cut a 1"x12" strip of tan vellum. She tore along the top edge, chalked the tear, placed it on the bottom edge and cut around the palm tree as shown. She tore the right edge of a 4"x11" rectangle of aqua vellum, chalked it and glued it to the left side of the page. She matted a 4"x6" photo on blue paper and glued it to the page. She cut an 8½"x9¼" rectangle of blue vellum, outlined it with the white pen and glued it over the photo as shown. She cut three 2" squares along the left side, and a 2¼"x3" rectangle ½" from the blue vellum and a 3"x½" rectangle along the bottom. She tore strips of tan vellum, chalked the edges and glued them to tan paper and covered the back of each window. She placed a photo in the largest window. She tore three more strips of tan vellum, chalked the edges and placed them on the page as shown. She outlined the window edges in white, then journaled with both pens and glued the shells, glass and sand in place.

- **patterned Paper Pizazz™:** palm tree collage (*Vacation Collage Papers*)
- **vellum Paper Pizazz™:** aqua, cornflower blue (*Pastel Vellum Papers*); tan (*Pastel Vellum Papers*, also by the sheet)
- **solid Paper Pizazz™:** cornflower blue (*Solid Muted Colors*); tan (*Plain Pastels*)
- **12" square of white foam core board:** Hunt Mfg. Co.
- **⅛" wide gold eyelets:** Stamp Studio
- **brown, aqua decorating chalks:** Craf-T Products

- **mini seashells:** U.S. Shell
- **sea glass**
- **white sand**
- **mini glue dots:** Glue Dots™ International LLC
- **X-acto® knife, cutting surface:** Hunt Mfg. Co.
- **white, black pens:** Sakura Gelly Roll
- **designer:** Lisa Garcia-Bergstedt

Cover the foam board with a 12"x8" of flourishes paper, then glue a 12"x4" of stripes on the bottom. Glue a 12"x¼" strip of gold along the top edge of the stripes piece. Place the foam on a cutting surface and use the knife to cut a 4⅛"x2" rectangle centered 1½" from the bottom edge and a 2½"x6" rectangle centered near the upper left corner. Cover the upper window back with gold and the lower with flourishes. Mat a 7" square of metallic gold border vellum on metallic gold and glue it near the upper right corner. Insert five snaps along the border as shown. Mat a photo on gold, leaving a ¼" border and glue it to the vellum as shown. With the remaining vellum, cut 2⅜"x5⅞" and 4⅛"x2" rectangles. Mat the first on gold, journal, then attach inside the upper window with a snap in each corner. Glue the embellishments inside the lower window.

- **patterned Paper Pizazz™:** gold/blue flourishes (*Metallic Gold*); gold/blue stripes, metallic gold (*Metallic Gold*, also by the sheet)
- **specialty Paper Pizazz™:** metallic gold border vellum (*Metallic Vellum*)
- **12" square of white foam core board:** Hunt Mfg. Co.
- **¼" wide silver snaps:** Making Memories

- **2" tall gold embellishments:** S. Axelrod Company
- **black pen:** Zig® Writer
- **designer:** Paris Dukes

Joy and Jason will always remember their honeymoon with this exotic page by Lisa. She matted the couple's photo on white and teal, then a layer of torn-edge sandstone and glued it to a rectangle of mosaic with a white mat. She glued it centered near the top of the blue ripple paper. She journaled on each of two sandstone rectangles, then matted each on white and used foam tape to attach them. She covered each foam square in mosaic, then matted each on white and teal. Lisa cut out a 1½" square from the center of two pieces and a 1" square from the center of the other. She glued them along a 2" torn-edge strip of sandstone. She used Tacky Tape™ to line the bottom of each window and poured sand onto the surface; then glued the shells inside. She cut letters from mosaic paper, matted each on sandstone and attached them with foam tape. She journaled with the black pen as shown.

- **patterned Paper Pizazz™:** mosaic, blue ripple (*Great Backgrounds*); sandstone (by the sheet)
- **solid Paper Pizazz™:** teal (*Solid Jewel Tones*); white (*Plain Pastels*)
- **2" squares of white foam core board:** Hunt Mfg. Co.
- **mini seashells:** US Shell
- **white sand**
- **schoolhouse letter die-cuts:** Accu/Cut® Systems
- **Terrifically Tacky Tape™:** Art Accents

- **foam adhesive tape:** Therm O Web
- **5mm, 15mm black pens:** Sakura Micron
- **X-acto® knife, cutting surface:** Hunt Mfg. Co.
- **designer:** Lisa Garcia-Bergstedt

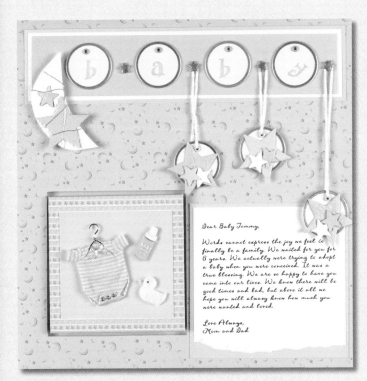

- **patterned Paper Pizazz™:** moons/stars, stars on stripes (*Mixing Baby Papers*)
- **solid Paper Pizazz™:** light yellow, light blue, white (*Plain Pastels*)
- **12" square of white foam core board:** Hunt Mfg. Co.
- **baby motifs:** Jolene's Boutique Stickers
- **eyelets:** Stamp Studio
- **silver star snaps, medium metal rimmed round tags:** Making Memories

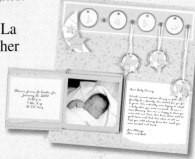

Congratulations Lisa La Centra! She tucked her precious bundle of joy into an adorable page— and inside a cutaway to reveal Tommy. Lisa covered the foam board with moon/stars paper, then used the knife to cut out the square in the lower left corner. She matted an 11"x2" blue strip onto white and yellow for the top banner, then attached round tags with eyelets. Between the tags, Lisa inserted star snaps on which she hung three tags covered in blue, white and yellow stars. She adorned the top left with a moon and stars wrapped with gold thread and white fiber. She cut a 9"x4½" of yellow, folded it in half and covered the front with stripes. She glued the baby motifs onto a 3¾" yellow square and glued it centered on the front. She glued Tommy's photo centered on the inside then attached the card inside the cutaway using foam tape. She journaled as shown. What a sweet page!

- **white fibers:** Adornaments™
- **gold thread:** DMC
- **paper stars:** Sizzix
- **Antiques Alphabet stamps, blue ink:** Stampin' Up!
- **foam adhesive tape:** Therm O Web
- **black pen:** Sakura Gelly Roll
- **designer:** Lisa La Centra

Here's a fun technique using vellum. Go ahead—crop and mat your photos, then place on your background page. Place a strip of vellum on top of the photo, then mark a window. Remove the vellum and use an X-acto® knife to cut out the window. Reposition on your page. Notice the vellum muted the photo but the window allows the subject to get extra attention. For another look, tear the window. You can add a peek-a-boo window to a photo, an area of the patterned paper, certain words in your journaling or on all three places! Try it....really, you'll like this new technique!

7 Shauna used the black pen to write the song lyrics. What a fun page to remember a fun day!

6 She tied charms along the fiber, then inserted the ends into the large eyelets. The gold charms match the gold eyelets and gold penwork.

5 She inserted a small eyelet at the ends of the vellums, then large eyelets centered on the top vellum.

4 She glued the last photo on the largest vellum and repeated the process for another window with the aqua vellum.

3 She placed the widest vellum even with the right side of the page and cut a 1⅝" square over Spencer's face then outlined it with gold pen.

2 She cut a 7½"x12" of baby blue, a 5¼"x12" of aqua and a 2½"x12" of sky blue vellum, then tore the left side of each.

1 Shauna chose a seashell collage paper to match the theme of her photos. She matted each photo on gold and used photo tinting pens to hightlight some things in each photo.

- **patterned Paper Pizazz™:** seashell collage (*Vacation Collage Papers*)
- **specialty Paper Pizazz™:** baby blue vellum, sky blue vellum, aqua vellum (*Pastel Vellum Papers*); gold (*Metallic Gold*, also by the sheet)
- **teal fibers:** Adornaments™
- **³⁄₁₆", ⅛" wide gold eyelets:** Stamp Studio
- **1⅝" wide gold starfish charms:** S. Axelrod Company
- **blue, yellow, peach, blush, honeycomb, light green photo tinting pens:** Zig® Photo Twin™
- **gold, black pens:** Sakura Gelly Roll
- **X-acto® knife, cutting surface:** Hunt Mfg. Co.
- **designer:** Shauna Berglund-Immel

Lisa took a peek into some of mother's special qualities with this page. She began with purple/black dots for a background, then journaled on a 2¾"x5" rectangle of dark lavender, matted on black. She cut 3⅜"x10⅝" from pansies and purple vellum. She glued the journaling near the bottom of the pansies with the vellum on top and traced rectangles around four words. She used the template to make a 2" square centered on a pansy. She cut out the windows and outlined each and the outer edge with gold pen. She glued the vellum on top of the pansies, then matted it on dark lavender and black. Lisa matted her photo on black, then dark lavender and glued it to a 7½"x11" of vellum and outlined the mat and vellum in gold. She placed a 7½"x3½" strip of vellum across the photo, traced and cut a window and outlined it and the outside edge in gold. She journaled on the vellum with both pens.

- **patterned Paper Pizazz™:** purple/black dots (*Bold & Bright*, also by the sheet); pansies (by the sheet)
- **vellum Paper Pizazz™:** pastel purple (*Pastel Vellum Papers*, also by the sheet)
- **solid Paper Pizazz™:** dark lavender, black (*Solid Jewel Tones*)
- **Paper Flair™ Windows #1 Template**
- **gold pen:** Sakura Gelly Roll
- **X-acto® knife, cutting surface:** Hunt Manufacturing Company
- **designer:** Lisa Garcia-Bergstedt

What better way to showcase rock-solid ideals than through Lisa's peek-a-boo windows! She matted her family photo on black and gray papers, then glued it to a rocks paper background. She placed the whole vellum sheet on top and used the template to draw three 1" and three 1½" squares centered on rocks and one 2¾" square centered on the faces in the photo. She used the knife to cut out the windows, then outlined each with the dark gray pen. She used the opaque black pen to write a word under each window and both pens for additional journaling. Rock, paper, scissors—they all win in this page!

- **patterned Paper Pizazz™:** rocks (by the sheet)
- **vellum Paper Pizazz™:** pastel tan (*Pastel Vellum Papers*, also by the sheet)
- **solid Paper Pizazz™:** gray, black (*Solid Jewel Tones*)
- **Paper Flair™ Windows #1 Template**
- **dark gray, black opaque, 8mm black pens:** Sakura Gelly Roll
- **X-acto® knife, cutting surface:** Hunt Mfg. Co.
- **designer:** Lisa Garcia-Bergstedt

A peek into each season through Griffin's eyes was patched together by Lisa in this delightful page. She tore out the moon from the Halloween collage paper, then glued it near the upper left corner of a 6" square from the same paper. She cut a 6" square from each remaining collage paper. Lisa stitched the squares together with gold floss. She matted one photo on black, one on lavender and two on blue. She tore a 5" square from each vellum and chalked the edges with a complimentary color. She used the template and knife to cut a different sized window into each vellum square then outlined each window with the gold pen. She journaled with the black pen on each vellum square.

- **patterned Paper Pizazz™:** Halloween, winter, spring, summer collage papers (*Holiday & Seasons Collage Papers*)
- **vellum Paper Pizazz™:** pastel peach, pastel blue, pastel purple (*Pastel Vellum Papers,* also by the sheet); white (by the sheet)
- **solid Paper Pizazz™:** light blue, lavender (*Solid Muted Colors*); black (*Solid Jewel Tones*)
- **Paper Flair™ Windows #1 Template**
- **¾" wide white snowflake charms**
- **blue, orange, purple decorating chalks:** Craf-T Products
- **gold embroidery floss, sewing needle:** DMC
- **gold, black pens:** Sakura Gelly Roll, Sakura Micron
- **X-acto® knife, cutting surface:** Hunt Mfg. Co.
- **designer:** Lisa Garcia-Bergstedt

Lisa centered on the family to make this peek-a-boo window page. She began with stripes for a background, then matted the photo on dark pink. Lisa cut a 6"x7½" pink vellum rectangle, tore and chalked the bottom edge, then cut a square window to frame the faces. She used the gold pen to outline the outer edges and to journal, then attached it to the page with snaps. She cut two 1½"x11" strips of paisley paper, matted one long edge of each on vellum and outlined the paper edge in gold. She cut 1½"x11" strips from each floral paper and tore each along one long edge, then matted each on vellum, tearing and chalking one long edge. She glued the strips as shown. She cut a vellum heart, matted it on paisley with torn edges, punched a hole on each top curve then outlined and journaled with the gold pen. She inserted wire through the holes, twisted the ends, hung the wire on the snap and used foam tape to adhere the heart to the page.

- **patterned Paper Pizazz™:** pink paisley stamps, pink flowers, pink stripes, pink floral (*Muted Tints*)
- **vellum Paper Pizazz™:** pastel pink (*Pastel Vellum Papers,* also by the sheet)
- **solid Paper Pizazz™:** dark pink (*Solid Jewel Tones*)
- **Paper Flair™ Windows #1 Template**
- **¼" wide dark pink snaps:** Making Memories
- **24-gauge dark pink wire:** Artistic Wire, Ltd.
- **pink decorating chalk:** Craf-T Products
- **⅛" wide hole punch:** Family Treasures
- **foam adhesive tape:** Therm O Web

- **gold pen:** Sakura Gelly Roll
- **X-acto® knife, cutting surface:** Hunt Mfg. Co.
- **designer:** Lisa Garcia-Bergstedt

Winter fun captured in a swirl of vellum, beads and fibers! Arlene cut three 13" fibers and attached them to the left side of the page. She made 15 beaded strings, varying in legnth from 1"-2". Arlene attached five to the top back of each tag. She punched snowflakes from white vellum and glued them to the back of the tags. Then she attached the tags on top of the fibers. She matted both photos on an 8"x11½" piece of pink vellum and placed a smaller 7½"x11" of light snowflake paper underneath. Arlene created the layered windows by placing a 5¾"x10¾" white vellum over the photos, then tore small windows as shown. She placed an 7½"x11" white vellum with the light snowflakes, then tore larger windows centered on each photo. Arlene computer journaled on a 7"x1½" white vellum strip and placed it between the photos. She attached the three layers of paper to the page with an eyelet in each corner. She added beaded borders at the top and bottom.

- **patterned Paper Pizazz™:** dark blue snowflake, light snowflake (*Swirls & Twirls*)
- **vellum Paper Pizazz™:** 2 sheets of white vellum (by the sheet), pink vellum (*Pastel Vellum Papers,* also by the sheet)
- **vellum tags, pewter square eyelets:** Making Memories™
- **small, medium, large snowflake punches:** Family Treasures, Inc.
- **pink, white, blue seed beads, white, silver bugle beads:** Blue Moon Beads/Elizabeth Ward & Co., Inc.
- **pink, white fibers:** Adornaments™
- **gold thread:** DMC
- **designer:** Arlene Peterson

Arlene used unequal quadrants in this page with pink vellum on white paper on the background. She glued 4¾"x7⅝", 4¾"x3¾" and 6¼"x3¾" rectangles of small tulips paper as shown, with a 6¼"x7¾" of pink plaid in the lower right corner. Arlene matted each photo on white, leaving ⅛" borders. One was centered on the plaid and the other overlapped three rectangles. She computer journaled on white, then trimmed it to the width of the top left photo and centered it below. Arlene placed an 11½"x11¼" of pink vellum centered on the page and used the template to draw the peek-a-boo windows onto the vellum. She removed the vellum and cut out the windows, then outlined the edges with the pink pen. She placed the vellum back on the page and inserted an eyelet in each corner. Arlene cut three 1" pink plaid squares, one 1" pink tulips square and one 1" large tulip square. She matted one plaid and one tulips square on white, each with a ¹⁄₁₆" border and glued them as shown. She punched three scallop edge white squares and one pink vellum tulip. She arranged them at the top right of the page, overlapping as shown. What a very sweet page!

- **patterned Paper Pizazz™:** pink plaid, pink tulip, large pink/green tulip, small pink/green tulip (*Joy's Soft Collection of Papers*)
- **vellum Paper Pizazz™:** pastel pink vellum (*Pastel Vellum Papers,* also by the sheet)
- **solid Paper Pizazz™:** white (*Plain Pastel Papers*)
- **windows template:** Paper Flair™ Windows #1
- **1⅜" scallop edge square punch, tulip punch:** Marvy® Uchida
- **³⁄₁₆" white eyelets:** Stamp Studio
- **pink pen:** Pentel of America, Ltd.
- **adhesive foam tape:** Therm O Web
- **designer:** Arlene Peterson

Folded frames are perfect for highlighting a special photo—and they're easy to make. Would we have it any other way? Just follow the directions below for a fabulous frame. Try one in vellum, like Arlene's version below, or create a different look with patterned papers glued back-to-back.If your photo is smaller or larger, you'll need to readjust the size of paper. Have fun!

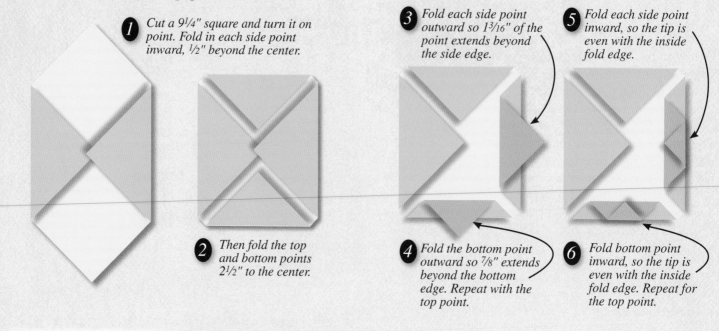

1 Cut a 9¼" square and turn it on point. Fold in each side point inward, ½" beyond the center.

2 Then fold the top and bottom points 2½" to the center.

3 Fold each side point outward so 1³⁄₁₆" of the point extends beyond the side edge.

4 Fold the bottom point outward so ⅞" extends beyond the bottom edge. Repeat with the top point.

5 Fold each side point inward, so the tip is even with the inside fold edge.

6 Fold bottom point inward, so the tip is even with the inside fold edge. Repeat for the top point.

5 Arlene created a folded frame from yellow floral vellum, (see directions above); then placed her photo matted on white on top of the frame.

4 Arlene glued the journaling mat centered on a 2¾"x9¼" rectangle of yellow vellum. She folded the yellow vellum ends onto the journal mat. Arlene cut a 1¾" yellow floral square, then cut it diagonally in half and glued a floral triangle at each end. Then she wrapped each vellum corner on top of the floral triangle and glued it in place.

1 Arlene chose yellow stripes for a background.

2 She cut a 9"x11" rectangle of yellow floral paper and matted it on yellow vellum, leaving a ¼" border. She placed it on the page at an angle, then trimmed the points even with the edges of the page.

3 Arlene computer journaled on a 2⅛"x7" white rectangle, then matted it on yellow floral paper, leaving ⅛" border on each side.

In the garden
of life, daughters
are the flowers
in bloom,
little by little,
day by day,
daughters
and flowers
grow that way.

Meagan
August 2002

- **patterned Paper Pizazz™:** yellow stripes, yellow floral, yellow floral vellum (*Joy's Garden*)
- **specialty Paper Pizazz™:** pastel yellow vellum (*Pastel Vellum Papers*, also by the sheet)
- **solid Paper Pizazz™:** white (*Plain Pastels*)
- **designer:** Arlene Peterson

Paris hung her ideas out for all to see in this tropical theme. She used blue flowers/green ferns patterned paper for a background, then attached a 12"x3¾" strip of blue flowers/green ferns vellum near the bottom edge with a snap in each corner. For the hammock, Paris glued a ¼"x2¼" strip of barnwood to each end of a 4½" long piece of mesh. She cut five 3½" lengths of twine, knotted the ends on one side with another twine piece, then glued the loose ends evenly spaced behind the mesh paper end; then repeated for the other side. For the pocket, Paris cut a 2½"x8¼" of patterned vellum, folded the bottom edge ⅝" under, then 1⅛" upward and attached the sides with a snap as shown. She inserted two glass pieces inside the pocket and one above as shown. She used the pen to journal along the pocket top. For the frame, Paris matted an 8"x6" rectangle of blue flowers on muted blue paper, leaving a 1/16" border. She cut a 7⅝"x6⅛" vellum rectangle, centered it on the floral piece, then folded each corner inward ¼" then outward. She inserted a snap to hold each corner. She matted the photo on blue and centered it in the frame.

- **patterned Paper Pizazz™**: blue flowers/green ferns, blue flowers on green, blue flowers/green ferns vellum (*Joy's Soft Collection*); barnwood (*Country*, also by the sheet)
- **solid Paper Pizazz™**: muted blue (*Soft Muted Colors*)
- **¼" wide blue snaps:** Making Memories
- **coastal light natural mesh, 3 pieces of ocean blues sea glass:** Magic Scraps
- **hemp twine**
- **glue dots:** Glue Dots™ International LLC
- **black pen:** Zig® Writer
- **designer:** Paris Dukes

Susan created a frame within a frame for this exquisite page. She began with purple dots for a background, then cut floral paper in half diagonally and matted it on silver with a 1/16" border on the diagonal edge and a ¼" mat of lavender vellum. She glued it even with the bottom edge of the background page. Susan cut a 3⅝"x12" of purple flowers vellum, used the silver pen to outline the edges, glued it centered on a 2⅝"x12" lavender paper, then glued the piece centered on the page. She cut an 11" square of lavender vellum, then 8" and 3⅝" squares of purple flowers vellum and followed the directions on page 108 to make folded frames of each. She cut ⅛" strips of silver to line the top and bottom of the large vellum frame and to wrap two corners of the small frame. She matted the photo on lavender, outlined it in silver and glued it on the frame. She journaled on a 2" lavender square, then inserted it into the small frame. She strung beads on wire, curled them, then glued them to the page as shown.

- **patterned Paper Pizazz™**: small purple floral, purple dots, purple flowers vellum (*Joy's Garden*)
- **specialty Paper Pizazz™**: pink-lavender vellum (*Pastel Vellum Papers*); metallic silver (*Metallic Silver*, also by the sheet)
- **solid Paper Pizazz™**: dark lavender (*Plain Pastels*)
- **lavender seed beads:** Blue Moon Beads/Elizabeth Ward & Co., Inc.
- **24-gauge silver wire:** Artistic Wire, Ltd.
- **⅛" wide hole punch:** Marvy® Uchida
- **violet, silver pens:** Sakura Gelly Roll
- **wire cutters, pliers**
- **designer:** Susan Cobb

Arlene has this page all folded up in stitches! She cut a ½"x11½" silver strip and traced the pattern below nine times. She started from the bottom and stitched the pattern with floss. She matted it on dot vellum, purple floral and silver again. She cut a 7"x10¼" purple floral rectangle and matted it on silver. Arlene centered the embroidered strip and the rectangle on the background. She cut an 8" square of dot vellum for the folded frame (see page 108). She matted the 3¾"x5¼" photo on silver, then centered it on top of the folded frame. Arlene computer journaled on silver paper, trimmed it to 4"x1¼" and double-matted it on purple floral then silver paper.

- **patterned Paper Pizazz™:** lavender floral, purple floral (*Swirls & Twirls*)
- **specialty Paper Pizazz™:** dot vellum (by the sheet), metallic silver (*Metallic Silver,* also by the sheet)
- **purple satin embroidery floss:** DMC
- **designer:** Arlene Peterson

Arlene captured the stars to create this sweet, fun page! She cut two 6" vellum squares and folded them into frames (see page 108). She punched 24 gold stars and attached three to each side of both frames. She cropped the photos to 2¾" squares and centered them in the frames. Arlene accentuated the frames placing them on 4¾" gold squares turned on point. She matted the cut-out tags on gold paper. Arlene balanced the page with the tag placement—attached with foam tape—then added a 12" length of ribbon to the right side of the page and a 9" length to the left side. She tied two small ribbon bows placed on top of each tag—a great finishing touch! She computer journaled on vellum, then cut them into star shapes to fit on the tags. A stellar page!

- **patterned Paper Pizazz™:** blue star (*Jacie's Watercolor Naturals*)
- **specialty Paper Pizazz™:** pastel blue vellum (*12"x12" Pastel Vellum Papers,* also by the sheet), metallic gold (*Metallic Gold,* also by the sheet)
- **tags:** *Paper Pizazz™ Tag Art #2*
- **¼" star punch:** Family Treasures, Inc.
- **gold ribbon:** C.M. Offray & Son, Inc.
- **adhesive foam tape:** Therm O Web
- **designer:** Arlene Peterson

Arlene "rose" to the challenge when creating this richly textured page! She cut the rose paper in half and placed it over the right side of the stripe paper. She cut a 9½"x8¼" of sponged paper and matted it on silver. Arlene balanced the page with an 11⅝"x2" leaves strip, matted on silver. She cut a 10" vellum square, edged it with the silver pen and folded it into the frame (see page 108). She made her own photo corners out of four 1"x2" leaves rectangles matted on silver. She folded each into a triangle, then wrapped it around a corner of the sponged paper. Arlene computer journaled on vellum, trimmed it to 4⅛"x1⅝", matted it on leaves and silver papers. She cropped each photo to 3"x4½" and matted both on one piece of silver paper, leaving ⅛" between. A beautiful setting for precious photos.

- **patterned Paper Pizazz™:** lavender stripe, lavender roses, lavender sponged, lavender leaves (*Joy's Vintage Collection*)
- **specialty Paper Pizazz™:** white vellum (by the sheet), metallic silver (*Metallic Silver,* also by the sheet)
- **silver pen:** Pentel of America, Ltd.
- **designer:** Arlene Peterson

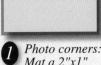

1 *Photo corners: Mat a 2"x1" rectangle on silver.*

2 *Fold the left corner to the back.*

3 *Fold the right corner to the back.*

Something old, something new, something borrowed, something blue. Arlene was inspired by tradition when she created this page! She tore a 3" wide strip of blue floral paper and attached it to the right side of the light blue floral background. She tore a 2½"-4" of vellum and attached it to the top of the page. Arlene made the folded frame with an 8" vellum square (see page 108) and outlined the edges with the gold pen. She matted the photo on gold and centered it on top of the frame. She journaled "Karey Ann" on the blue vellum at the top of the page then "Love," "Honor" and "Cherish" on 1¾"x1" vellums. She outlined the vellums with gold pen then double-matted the three words on blue floral and gold papers. Arlene placed the charms between the journal blocks then added a metallic bow at the top of each. She used the ribbon to tie a sheer bow and placed it above the frame. So very pretty!

- **patterned Paper Pizazz™:** light blue floral, blue floral (*Flowered "Handmade" Papers*)
- **specialty Paper Pizazz™:** pastel blue vellum (*12"x12" Pastel Vellum Papers,* also by the sheet), metallic gold (*Metallic Gold,* also by the sheet)
- **⅛" wide gold metallic ribbon:** C.M. Offray & Son, Inc.
- **⅝" wide sheer gold ribbon:** Horizon Fabric, Inc.
- **gold heart charms:** S. Axelrod Company
- **gold pen:** Pentel of America, Ltd.
- **designer:** Arlene Peterson

The effect may look worn—but distressing adds warmth and sophistication to papers and embellishments on your page. Shauna used chalk to create a well-traveled effect on her page below. Arlene crumpled metallic paper, Toddi used water and salt on vellum, Susan used a hammer and sandpaper then Paris swabbed embossing foil with black ink for distressing techniques. Each creates a spectacular effect befitting their theme. So, go ahead and "age" your page. It's a modern way to the past!

7 She cut various stamps and stickers, then used the gold pen to draw dashes along the belts, photo mats and page sides.

6 She inserted an eyelet in the large rectangle and tag then connected the two pieces and the key charm with black floss.

5 Shauna journaled on an ivory tag and two rectangles, then chalked each brown. She matted the large rectangle on black, speckled and gold then outlined the two smaller pieces with a black pen.

4 She matted her photo on gold, speckled, then on a large mat of "handmade" brown, speckled and gold then attached it to the page with a small brad in each corner.

3 Shauna cut two buckles from gold, matted them on black and glued one near the top of each belt. She wrapped a gold matted strip of brown on speckled around each belt. She attached two eyelets below the buckle, then a brad at the bottom of each belt.

1 Shauna chalked the "handmade" brown paper with black for the background. She cut two ¼" strips of speckled paper, matted one long side on gold and glued one to each side of the page.

2 She matted two 7" and two 5½" lengths of ½" wide strips of "handmade" brown onto gold, then speckled and again on gold. She glued one of each size to form a belt on each side of the page.

- **patterned Paper Pizazz™:** gold speckled on brown (*Spattered, Crackled & Sponged*); handmade brown (*"Handmade" Papers*); stamps, travel stickers (*Vacation #2, also by the sheet*)
- **specialty Paper Pizazz™:** gold (*Metallic Gold*)
- **solid Paper Pizazz™:** black (*Solid Jewel Tones*); ivory (*Plain Pastels*)
- **Paper Pizazz™ Charms Punch-Outs™:** gold key
- **3/16" gold eyelets:** Stamp Studio
- **¼", ⅛" gold brads:** AmericanPin/ Hyglo®
- **gold thread, black embroidery floss, sewing needle:** DMC
- **brown, black decorating chalks:** Craf-T Products
- **gold pen:** Sakura Gelly Roll
- **black pen:** Zig® Millenium
- **tracing paper, transfer paper**
- **designer:** Shauna Berglund-Immel
- **photo:** courtesy of INVU Photography by Helen

Arlene aged the papers on this heritage page to fit the feel of the photograph. She cut three 12"x2½" gold strips, crumpled them and smoothed them out again. She lightly sanded each strip to roughen and age it then matted each on black. She placed them evenly spaced on the stripes background and attached them with an eyelet in each corner. Arlene added the 7½"x11" black mat to balance the page. She cut a 7½"x11" piece of tile paper, tore each edge and chalked. She crumpled, smoothed and sanded it. She attached it to the black mat with a gold snap in each corner. She photocopied the photo, tore the edges and chalked. She matted it on black then gold and centered at the top of the tile paper. She computer journaled on gold and trimmed it to 3⅝"x1¼". Arlene tied the journaling to the rest of the page when she matted it on black and gold the same width as the photo.

- **patterned Paper Pizazz™:** gold, gold/black stripe, gold tile (*Metallic Gold*)
- **solid Paper Pizazz™:** black (*Solid Jewel Tones*)
- **tan, black decorating chalks:** Craf-T Products
- **¼" gold snaps:** Making Memories™
- **⅛" black eyelets:** Stamp Studio
- **designer:** Arlene Peterson

Susan softened this rustic photo with a few distressing techniques. She used sandpaper to randomly scuff the torn 8½"x10" ivory background paper, which was glued to its companion sheet of tan "handmade". She matted her photo on pink and glued it to ivory vellum, then tore the edges. Susan glued the photo slightly overlapping a 4¾"x7" torn edge rectangle of tan vellum, a 6¾"x7¾" torn edge rectangle of ivory vellum turned on point and an 8"x2" torn edge strip of ivory. She tore two 1½"-2" squares each of tan vellum, white vellum and mauve paper then glued them overlapping in groups of three on the page as shown. Susan sanded the buttons, threaded each with floss, knotting the ends at the back, then glued them to the squares. Susan chalked the edges of each vellum piece and used the pen to journal.

- **patterned Paper Pizazz™:** mauve/tan handmade, mauve/ivory handmade (*Flowered "Handmade" Papers*)
- **specialty Paper Pizazz™:** tan vellum (*Pastel Vellum Papers*, also by the sheet); ivory, white vellums (by the sheet)
- **solid Paper Pizazz™:** mauve (*Solid Muted Colors*)
- **mauve, pink buttons:** Magic Scraps
- **pink embroidery floss:** DMC
- **pink, brown, lavender decorating chalks:** Craf-T Products
- **fine grade sandpaper**
- **black pen:** Zig® Writer
- **designer:** Susan Cobb

Grandma's Violin... Grandma's Girl

Shii Ann before her Holiday Recital, December 2001

flag pattern

Paris performed a masterpiece in this exquisite page. She began with a burgundy collage background. She tore an 8"x9" rectangle of white vellum, crumped it, smoothed it out, then applied gold chalk along the edges. She centered it on the right side of the page and inserted a brad in each corner. She cropped her photo to 6½"x4½" and matted it on the solid burgundy, leaving a ¼" border. She cut a 7½"x5½" rectangle of gold, crumpled it, smoothed it out, then glued the photo on top. She attached gold photo corners, then glued it to the page as shown. Paris used glue dots to adhere the ribbon rose, charm and pearls to the lower left corner of the page as shown. She used the pen to journal along the lace and below the photo. How lovely!

- **patterned Paper Pizazz™:** lace border burgundy collage (*Jacie's Collage Papers*)
- **specialty Paper Pizazz™:** metallic gold (*Metallic Gold*, also by the sheet); white vellum (by the sheet)
- **solid Paper Pizazz™:** burgundy (*Solid Muted Tints*)
- **gold violin charm:** S. Axelrod Company
- **1" wide burgundy satin ribbon rose:** C.M. Offray & Son, Inc.
- **gold photo corners:** Canson-Talens, Inc.
- **⅛" wide gold brads:** Magic Scraps
- **metallic gold chalk:** Craf-T Products
- **fused pearls:** Hirschberg Shultz & Company
- **foam adhesive tape:** Therm O Web
- **black pen:** Zebra Jimnie Gel Rollerball
- **glue dots:** Glue Dots™ International LLC
- **designer:** Paris Dukes

Ship Ahoy! Toddi caught the moment and a wave in this seaworthy page. She began the voyage with a green plaid background, then matted two photos each on brown, leaving a 1⁄16" border and glued them centered on the page. She traced the flag pattern onto white vellum and glued it between the two photos. She cut a ¼"x1½" of brown for the flag pole, glued it to the left of the vellum flag, then used the black pen to journal and draw dots and lines between the shapes. She placed the green vellum on a cutting surface and used the knife to cut a 7½"x10" window in the center. Toddi created this unusual distressing effect by dripping water onto the vellum frame then sprinkling salt on top. She used the hair dryer to dry the frame, then glued it to the page. It's a page fit for the captain's quarters!

- **patterned Paper Pizazz™:** green plaid (*Mixing Masculine Papers*)
- **specialty Paper Pizazz™:** pastel green vellum (*Pastel Vellum Papers*, also by the sheet); white vellum (by the sheet)
- **solid Paper Pizazz™:** brown (*Solid Jewel Tones*)
- **hair dryer**
- **water**
- **salt**
- **black pen:** Sakura Gelly Roll
- **X-acto® knife, cutting surface:** Hunt Mfg. Co.
- **designer:** Toddi Barclay

Wooden Yacht Club ~ Seattle ~ June 2000

Susan captured the "golden age" to feature this heirloom photo. She used tan swirls paper for a background, then glued a 12"x2" of tan vellum (torn along the top and bottom edges) across the center of the page. Susan cut a 7½"x12" of ivory swirls, then tore each side. She cut along the edge of the laser lace scallops, glued it to the left side of the ivory swirls back, then glued the piece centered on the page. She tore a 5½"x8" tan vellum, placed it on the mouse pad and used the hammer to pound an "aged" effect into it. She cut a 5½"x4½" of gold, tore it along the left and right sides, then applied the hammer treatment to it. She matted her photo on tan paper, tore the edges, then secured it to the page with an eyelet in each corner. She used the sandpaper to distress the eyelets, then chalked the photo mat and laser lace. She tied thread through the eyelets. She used the gold pen to trace a few swirls and to journal. So lovely, Susan!

- **patterned Paper Pizazz™:** tan swirls & twirls, ivory swirls & twirls (*Swirls & Twirls*)
- **specialty Paper Pizazz™:** tan vellum (*Pastel Vellum Papers*, also by the sheet); metallic gold (*Metallic Gold*, also by the sheet); laser lace (by the sheet)
- **solid Paper Pizazz™:** light tan (*Plain Pastels*)
- **⅛" wide brown eyelets:** Stamp Studio
- **metallic gold thread:** Westrim® Crafts
- **dark brown, light brown decorating chalks; metallic copper chalk:** Craf-T Products
- **gold pen:** Sakura Gelly Roll
- **fine grade sandpaper**
- **hammer, computer mouse pad**
- **designer:** Susan Cobb

Like a good saddle, embossed metal wears well. Paris used teal floral embossed "leather" for a background. She cut 3"x6", 8"x6⅛" and 12"x2" pieces of gold foil, then used the tracing wheel along the edges. She dabbed the pen onto the swab then wiped the swab across the foil for an aged look. She attached the metal with glue dots. She attached the stars and horseshoe to a length of wire, curled it between the charms, then glued them to a torn edge and chalked 10"x3½" teal leather rectangle. Paris matted her photo on teal and black, then on a torn edge 7½"x5½" rectangle of teal flowers/dots "embossed" and glued it to the large gold foil piece. She matted the boot on a 1½"x2⅜" flowers/dots piece, matted it on black and glued it to a torn edge 2½"x5¼" teal rectangle. She added stars as shown.

- **patterned Paper Pizazz™:** teal floral "embossed", teal flowers/dots "embossed", teal "leather" (*"Leather" Papers*)
- **solid Paper Pizazz™:** black (*Solid Jewel Tones*)
- **ArtEmboss™ medium weight gold foil, wood embossing tool:** American Art Clay Co., Inc.
- **1½", ⅝", ⁷⁄₁₆" wide stars; 1¼" cowboy boot; ½" wide horseshoe brass charms:** S. Axelrod Company
- **24-gauge gold wire:** Colour Craft™
- **black decorating chalk:** Craf-T Products
- **tracing wheel:** Dritz
- **adhesive foam tape:** Therm O Web
- **glue dots:** Glue Dots™ International LLC
- **black pen:** Sakura Permapaque
- **computer mouse pad**
- **cotton swab**
- **wire cutters**
- **designer:** Paris Dukes

Embossing on metal creates an exciting new look to your scrapbook pages. Aluminum, brass and copper are readily available in most craft stores and come in a variety of thicknesses. You may have to hunt for the colored varieties, but they are worth it. There are a few basic tools you'll need to make embossing fun and easy—a computer mouse pad and a wooden stylus are a must! The "give" in the mouse pad is perfect for allowing the metal to receive the impression from the stylus. Wooden tools won't scratch the soft metal, as metal tools might. For more fun, try punches with the softer embossing metals, as Paris did on page 117. For lettering, first lightly trace each letter onto the metal, then turn the piece over and press into the metal to achieve a raised effect. If you want the imprint to sink into the metal, try a non-water based ink to fill in the imprints as Susan did on page 119. For a sophisticated look, repeat the pattern on your patterned paper onto the metal, as Susan did with the fern below. (She traced the pattern onto tracing paper to use for the embossing.) Any way you work it, your embossed metal will provide a stunning addition to your pages.

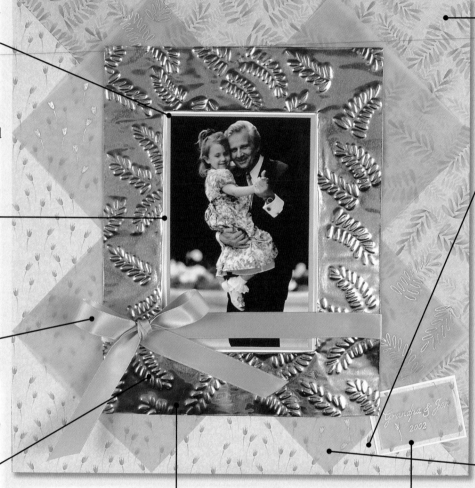

8 She glued the photo centered on the page, then glued the frame centered on top.

7 She cropped the photo to 3½"x5⅝" and matted it on lavender then white papers, each with a ¹⁄₁₆" border. She wrapped the ribbon around the frame and tied the ends into a bow.

6 Susan traced the fern pattern onto tracing paper, then placed it on the frame back side and used the wooden stylus to press the pattern into the aluminum in random angles.

5 Susan cut a 7"x9" rectangle from the aluminum foil, then placed it on a cutting surface and used the knife to cut a 3⅞"x5⅞" rectangle in the center to form a frame.

4 She used the pen to journal on a 2"x1¼" vellum rectangle, matted it on lavender tulips then white paper.

1 Susan began with a lavender ferns patterned paper for a background.

2 She cut the tulips paper in half diagonally, then glued one piece even with the bottom edge.

3 Susan cut two 5"x11⅝" rectangles of lavender vellum, then overlapped them in a "X" on the page. She used the silver pen to trace some patterns under the vellum.

- **patterned Paper Pizazz™:** lavender ferns, lavender tulips, lavender sponged vellum (*Joy's Soft Collection of Papers*)
- **solid Paper Pizazz™:** muted lavender (*Solid Muted Colors*); white (*Plain Pastels*)
- **ArtEmboss™ medium weight aluminum foil, wood embossing tool:** American Art Clay Co., Inc.
- **32" of ⅝" wide lavender satin ribbon:** C.M. Offray & Son, Inc.
- **silver pen:** Sakura Gelly Roll
- **X-acto® knife, cutting surface:** Hunt Mfg. Co.
- **computer mouse pad**
- **tracing paper**
- **designer:** Susan Cobb

Autumn in its most vibrant moment—captured with embossing metal forever! Paris began with green "embossed" leaves paper for a background. She matted her photo on green "leather" paper, leaving 1/8" border; then on copper, leaving a 1/16" border. She matted the photo once more on green "leather", leaving a 1/4" border. She die-cut one copper and two green oak leaves; four green and five copper mini leaves. She used the embossing tool to imprint the veins, then used glue dots to attach them to the page. Susan cut 1" wide rectangles of green foil and embossed Natalie's name and the year. She cut a 3"x1½" green foil piece, trimmed the right corners, then punched a hole into the right end. She embossed "fall" into the tag, then inserted 8" of ribbon and knotted it. She wrapped the remaining ribbon around the oak leaf stems and tied it into a shoestring bow. Such a shining page!

- **patterned Paper Pizazz™:** green "embossed" leaves, green "leather" (*"Leather" Papers*)
- **specialty Paper Pizazz™:** metallic copper (*Heavy Metal Papers*)
- **ArtEmboss™ medium weight copper, mint green foils; wood embossing tool:** American Art Clay Co., Inc.
- **copper photo corners:** Canson-Talens, Inc.
- **gift tag #3, mini leaves, oak leaf #2 die-cuts:** Accu/Cut® Systems
- **24" of 5/8" wide ivory sheer ribbon:** C.M. Offray & Son, Inc.
- **1/8" wide hole punch:** Marvy® Uchida
- **foam adhesive tape:** Therm O Web
- **glue dots:** Glue Dots™ International LLC
- **computer mouse pad**
- **designer:** Paris Dukes

She embedded love into your heart—what better way than have it embedded into your page! Arlene chose pink hearts/swirls paper for a background. She matted a 10⅝"x7⅜" of dark pink hearts/swirls onto silver, leaving a 1/8" border, then inserted an eyelet in each corner. She cut one 2"x7" and two 2"x2½" rectangles from the foil. She punched a large heart and swirl from scrap paper; then used them on the back side of each 2½" foil piece to emboss the designs. She placed the letters to spell "love" on the back side of the long foil piece and repeated the embossing technique, then used the tracing wheel to emboss the edges. She attached the foil with foam tape. She cut six ½" foil squares and punched a small heart in each. She hung the squares from floss inserted through the eyelets and glued the hearts as shown. She matted the photo on silver, journaled on silver and used the wheel around each edge. A floss bow tops off the journaling.

- **patterned Paper Pizazz™:** pink hearts/swirls, dark pink hearts/swirls (*Swirls & Twirls*)
- **specialty Paper Pizazz™:** metallic silver (*Metallic Silver,* also by the sheet)
- **ArtEmboss™ medium weight aluminum foil, wood embossing tool:** American Art Clay Co., Inc.
- **pink, silver embroidery floss:** DMC
- **tracing wheel:** Dritz
- **5/16", 1⅛" wide heart punches:** Family Treasures, Inc.
- **5/8" wide swirl punch:** Marvy® Uchida
- **"Classic Caps" letter template:** Frances Meyer, Inc.
- **3/16" silver eyelets:** Stamp Studio
- **adhesive foam tape:** Therm O Web
- **computer mouse pad, scrap paper**
- **designer:** Arlene Peterson

Embossed metal in nested shapes—what a stunning combination! Susan used the brown collage for a background, then created dimension in the tag (which is part of the paper) by inserting a copper eyelet at the top and threading fibers inside. She used the template to cut 1-D and 3-D shapes from the copper foil and 2-D from the aluminum. She used the embossing tool to imprint dots and swirls into the foil shapes, then layered 3-D onto 2-D and punched a hole in the center. She inserted the brad into the hole and attached it to the tag bottom. Susan tore a rectangle from each vellum, overlapped them at random angles and glued them centered on the page, then added 1-D shape as shown. She matted the photo on silver then glued ¼" copper foil strips to the photo corners, trimming the ends even with the silver mat, then glued it to the page center. She used the copper pen to journal. What a stunning combination!

- **patterned Paper Pizazz™:** brown stamp/tag collage (*Jacie & Joy's Collage Papers*)
- **specialty Paper Pizazz™:** vellum dots (*Vellum Papers*, also by the sheet); tan vellum (*Pastel Vellum Papers*, also by the sheet); ivory vellum (by the sheet); metallic silver (*Metallic Silver*, also by the sheet)
- **Paper Flair™ Nested Shapes Template**
- **ArtEmboss™ light weight copper, aluminum foils, wood embossing tool:** American Art Clay Co., Inc.
- **¼" wide copper eyelet:** Stamp Studio
- **⅛" wide silver brad:** AmericanPin/Hyglo®
- **tan, metallic copper fibers:** Adornaments™
- **1/16" wide hole punch:** McGill, Inc.
- **foam adhesive tape:** Therm O Web
- **copper pen:** Sakura Gelly Roll
- **computer mouse pad**
- **designer:** Susan Cobb

Rustic letter tiles and embossed leaves complement the natural setting of the photo. Arlene cut an 8½"x3½" of green leaves/flowers and matted it on vellum. She placed it in the top left corner of the page. She cut a 3"x8½" piece of green leaves/flowers and matted it on green. She placed it in the bottom right corner and let the corners overlap. Arlene made an embossing pattern from scrap cardstock punched in a leaf of each size. She embossed the large leaf on four 1"x2" metal rectangles and the small leaf on two ¾"x1¼" rectangles. She used the tracing wheel to outline the edges. Arlene punched one large and two small leaves from metal and embossed the veins. She cut out each letter tile and mounted them with foam tape arranging metal tiles among the letters. She matted the photo on silver, green leaves/flowers and vellum with an extra 2" on the left side. She computer journaled on vellum, then trimmed and placed it over the vellum mat. Arlene used the fibers as borders at the top and the bottom of the page and in knots around the journaling. A lovely setting!

- **patterned Paper Pizazz™:** light green leaves/flowers, green leaves/flowers (*Flowered "Handmade" Papers*)
- **specialty Paper Pizazz™:** pastel green vellum (*Pastel Vellum Papers,* also by the sheet), metallic silver (*Metallic Silver,* also by the sheet)
- **ArtEmboss™ medium weight aluminum foil, wood embossing tool:** American Art Clay Co., Inc.
- **alphabet cut-outs:** *Artsy Collage™ Alphabet Tiles*
- **green fibers:** Adornaments™
- **tracing wheel:** Dritz
- **small, large leaf punch:** Family Treasures, Inc.
- **adhesive foam tape:** Therm O Web
- **designer:** Arlene Peterson

A wonderful collection of blue papers complement Rick's shirt. Arlene made the bottom border with a 12"x2" strip of vellum that she matted on blue lines and white papers. For the metal, she punch six scalloped squares and cut one in half with scallop scissors. She used the stencil to emboss the squiggle lines on each piece. (Notice they match the lines paper.) She cut seven 1¼" white squares, four 1" blue gingham squares and four 1" blue stripe squares. Arlene cut the gingham and stripe squares in half, then matted one of each on the white squares. She matted the photo on white, then on a 7¼"x7⅝" piece of vellum. She matted the vellum on blue lines, vellum and white paper. Arlene computer journaled on vellum and trimmed it to 1¼"x5¾". She matted it on a 1¾"x7½" piece of blue lines and then on white. She arranged the metal and white squares in an alternating pattern.

- **patterned Paper Pizazz™:** blue check, blue lines, blue stripe, blue gingham (*Mixing Masculine Papers*)
- **vellum Paper Pizazz™:** blue vellum (*Pastel Vellum Papers*, also by the sheet)
- **solid Paper Pizazz™:** white (*Plain Pastels*)
- **ArtEmboss™ medium weight aluminum foil, wood embossing tool:** American Art Clay Co., Inc.
- **1⅜" scallop edge square punch:** Marvy® Uchida
- **scallop decorative scissors:** Fiskars®
- **small squiggle template:** Fresh and Funky Mini Stencils
- **designer:** Arlene Peterson

(See page 128 for the companion page.)

- **patterned Paper Pizazz™:** pink roses, sage tiles, pink monochromatic floral (*Joy's Vintage Papers*)
- **specialty Paper Pizazz™:** pink vellum (*Pastel Vellum Papers*, also by the sheet); white vellum (by the sheet); metallic silver (*Metallic Silver*, also by the sheet)
- **solid Paper Pizazz™:** ivory (*Plain Pastels*)
- **templates:** Paper Flair™ Tags, Windows #1

Susan prepared the finest silver to adorn this bridal setting. She used pink floral for the background, then glued a 10"x11½" of pink vellum centered along the bottom edge. She matted a 7¾"x9¾" of sage tiles onto ivory, leaving a 1/16" border; then onto white vellum, leaving an 1/8" border. She glued it to the center of the vellum. Susan matted the photo on silver. Susan used the knife to cut out the roses and butterflies then glued it to the page as shown. She used the template to cut a tag and two 1" squares of foil, then cut the squares diagonally in half. She applied the stencil to the foils, then dabbed the swab into pink ink and spread it onto the stenciling, using alcohol to remove the ink outside the stenciling. She punched a hole in the tag top, inserted the ribbon and tied it into a shoestring bow. She journaled on ivory, matted on silver and pink vellum as shown. How lovely! For a companion page, see page 128.

- **ArtEmboss™ light weight aluminum foil, wood embossing tool:** American Art Clay Co., Inc.
- **rose brass stencils:** American Traditions Stencils
- **20" of ⅞" wide pink sheer ribbon:** C.M. Offray & Son, Inc.
- **¼" wide hole punch:** Marvy® Uchida
- **pink pen:** Sakura Permapaque
- **silver pen:** Sakura Gelly Roll
- **rubbing alcohol, tissues**
- **cotton swab**
- **computer mouse pad**
- **X-acto® knife, cutting surface:** Hunt Mfg. Co.
- **designer:** Susan Cobb

Fabulous frames are a fantastic way to feature your precious photos with artistic flair! You can form a frame as easily as cutting a window into a patterned paper matted on vellum (as Shauna did on page 121), or create an eloborate tapestry with papers, vellums and embellishments as shown in the fall leaves page on page 122. Layering papers creates depth in the frame. Adding eyelets, embroidery floss and metallic thread provide a practical way to secure the frame to the page and add whimsy to your frame. Let's take a look.

7 The tan vellum was glued to the tan rectangle, then the frame centered on top.

8 For continuity, the gold pen was used for journaling on the peach vellum.

6 A black and white photo of Kaelin was glued to the back of the window. Foam tape was used to attach one small and two large leaves to the lower right corner.

1 A tan/brown watercolor plaid sets the stage for this autumn scene.

2 Lisa cut an 8" square each of peach paper and peach vellum, then a 7"x8¾" rectangle each of tan paper and tan vellum. She used the gold pen to outline each vellum piece.

5 Lisa placed the leaves rectangle on a cutting surface, then used a ruler and pencil to lightly draw a 3⅜"x5" window in the center, with straight lines only along the upper right side, and small portions along the top between the leaf edges. She used the knife to cut along the leaves and straight lines, then outlined the edges in gold.

3 She cut a 6⅜"x8" rectangle of fall leaves, then cut three large and three small individual leaves.

4 One large leaf was glued to the upper left corner of the peach rectangle, with a small leaf in the upper right and lower left corners. The peach vellum was placed on top of the peach paper, then an eyelet was inserted in each top corner and two 2¼" apart in the lower left corner. Gold floss was inserted into the eyelet pairs, with the ends glued at the back.

- **patterned Paper Pizazz™**: fall leaves, tan/brown plaid (*Jacie's Watercolor Naturals*)
- **specialty Paper Pizazz™**: pastel peach vellum, tan vellum (*Pastel Vellum Papers*, also by the sheet)
- **solid Paper Pizazz™**: peach, tan (*Solid Muted Colors*)
- **⅛" wide gold eyelets**: Stamp Studio
- **metallic gold embroidery floss**: DMC
- **X-acto® knife, cutting surface**: Hunt Manufacturing Co.
- **foam adhesive tape**: Therm O Web
- **gold pen**: Sakura Gelly Roll
- **ruler, pencil**
- **designer**: Lisa Garcia-Bergstedt

Shauna gathered delicate flowers and vellums from *Joy's Garden* for this stunning page with a nested frame. She placed purple daisy vellum over purple stripes paper and inserted an eyelet in each corner. She cut a 7⅜"x12" rectangle of purple flowers and used the knife to cut the 5"x6½" and 5"x1½" windows. She matted it on purple vellum with ⅛" borders on each side and inside the large window. Then she outlined the borders and windows with the gold pen. She centered the rectangle on the page and inserted an eyelet in each corner. She matted her photo on vellum and tore around the lavender tile edges. She inserted fibers from the back into the eyelets on each side of the photo mat and tied the ends in a shoestring bow.

- **patterned Paper Pizazz™:** purple flowers, purple stripes, purple daisy vellum (*Joy's Garden*)
- **vellum Paper Pizazz™:** pastel purple (*Pastel Vellum Papers*, also by the sheet)
- **alphabet cut-outs:** *Artsy Collage™ Alphabet Tiles*
- **⅛" wide gold eyelets:** Stamp Studio
- **yellow fiber:** Adornaments™
- **gold pen:** Sakura Gelly Roll
- **X-acto® knife, cutting surface:** Hunt Mfg. Co.
- **designer:** Shauna Berglund-Immel

Lisa lassoed this cowboy's dream into a fabulous folded frame. She used denim for the background paper. She matted her photo on black, then on tan with a 1" border. Lisa cut the plaid paper 2" larger than the tan mat, then cut a 1" slit into each corner. She wrapped it onto the photo mat. She inserted star brads along the plaid border. Lisa glued the frame to the page, then inserted an eyelet ½" from each corner. She threaded twine through the eyelets, gluing the ends at the back. She glued the alphabet tiles along a 16" length of twine, knotted it once on each side, inserted a star onto each end and wrapped the ends to the back. She used the black pens for journaling.

- **patterned Paper Pizazz™:** 12"x12" denim, red tartan (by the sheet)
- **solid Paper Pizazz™:** tan, black (*Solid Jewel Tones*)
- **alphabet cut-outs:** *Artsy Collage™ Alphabet Tiles*
- **¼" wide gold eyelets:** Stamp Studio
- **1" aluminum star tags, ⁵⁄₁₆" aluminum star brads:** Making Memories® Details™
- **hemp twine**
- **foam adhesive tape:** Therm O Web
- **black pens:** Sakura Micron, Opaque
- **designer:** Lisa Garcia-Bergstedt

Lisa framed Travis and Trea's affirmations of love with fabulous heart frame bags for this romantic page. She matted a 10⅜"x10¾" stripes rectangle on white and attached it to the stars paper with a black eyelet in each corner. She cut her photo to 4"x6", matted it on red, then on white. She cut the corrugated paper to form a frame for the photo and inserted a red eyelet in each corner. Lisa strung heart and alpha beads onto hemp spelling "love letters", with a knot at each end. She journaled on white, matted on red and used foam tape to attach it below the photo. Lisa used the template and knife to cut a heart in each envelope, then on each head shot of the couple. She glued each heart photo on a tag so it would show in the window. She strung alpha beads to spell each name. She glued the envelopes to the page. She used the pen to write "for" on the envelope above each beaded name and outlined the hearts.

- **patterned Paper Pizazz™:** white stripes on red, white stars on red (*Stripes, Checks & Dots*)
- **solid Paper Pizazz™:** red (*Solid Jewel Tones*); white (*Solid Pastels Papers*)
- **heart:** *Paper Flair™ Windows #2 Template*
- **2½"x3¾" brown paper bags**
- **2¼"x3¾" dark red tags**
- **black corrugated paper**
- **red, black ⅛" eyelets:** Stamp Studio
- **¼" alpha beads:** Darice, Inc.
- **hemp twine**
- **foam adhesive tape:** Therm O Web
- **X-acto® knife, cutting surface:** Hunt Mfg. Co.
- **black pen:** Sakura Micron
- **designer:** Lisa Garcia-Bergstedt

Lisa formed a fabulous frame from torn-edge corners, eyelets and gold floss. She used burgundy feather paper for a background and covered the bottom with a 2½" wide strip of large leaves. She tore and chalked the top and bottom edges of a 3" strip of vellum, placed it on a 5" strip of small leaves, matted on tan paper, then tore and rolled along the bottom edge. She attached the mat to the page with two eyelets at each end and inserted gold floss through each set, gluing the ends at the back. She matted her photo on burgundy and tan. She cut four 1¾" squares of tan, tore each in half diagonally and slightly rolled the edges, then glued one to each photo corner. She inserted a pair of eyelets along each section of the tan mat, threaded floss through and glued the ends at the back. She cut out eight leaves from the large leaves paper and used foam tape to attach one to each photo corner and the rest on the page as shown. She journaled with the gold pen.

- **patterned Paper Pizazz™:** burgundy feather, small leaves on burgundy, large leaves on burgundy (*Mixing Jewel Pattern Papers*)
- **vellum Paper Pizazz™:** pastel tan (*Pastel Vellum Papers*, also by the sheet)
- **solid Paper Pizazz™:** light tan (*Solid Pastel Papers*); burgundy (*Solid Jewel Tones*)
- **3/16" gold eyelets:** Stamp Studio
- **gold embroidery floss:** DMC
- **brown decorating chalk:** Craf-T Products
- **foam adhesive tape:** Therm O Web
- **gold pen:** Sakura Gelly Roll
- **designer:** Lisa Garcia-Bergstedt

Those who plant love into the lives of others
cannot keep it from themselves.
Bonner, August 2002

Arlene captured the spirit of gardening in this peaceful page! She cut three 1½"x8" fern paper strips and two 1½"x8" blue flower paper strips then matted each on green vellum. She staggard them on the green/blue check background. Arlene cropped the photo to 6½"x4½". She cut a 7¾"x5½" piece of flower/fern vellum and matted it on green vellum. She tore out the center of both vellums, leaving the opening ½" larger on the side than she matted. She placed them on top of the photo and cut a slit in each corner and folded each edge back ½". The photo corners are ½" wide strips of green and flower/fern vellums wrapped around each corner. She computer journaled on green vellum and matted it on fern paper and green vellum. She added torn strips of flower/fern and green vellums for a repeating design element. So full of summer!

- **patterned Paper Pizazz™:** green/blue check, fern, flower/fern vellum (*Joy's Soft Collection of Papers*)
- **vellum Paper Pizazz™:** green vellum (*12"x12" Pastel Vellum Papers,* also by the sheet)
- **designer:** Arlene Peterson

Arlene brought this heritage photo up to date with unique matting and a funky frame! She cut a 10¾"x8¼" piece of blue leaves paper and matted it on solid blue. For the center strip, she cut a 10¾"x3" daisies paper, tore the edges and chalked them with blue. She cut two 26" lengths of each ribbon, overlapped them, then arranged them behind the large mat as shown, trimming the ends at an angle. Arlene matted the photo on solid blue then tore a frame from dot vellum, placed on top of the photo. She wrapped floss around the frame and tied a bow in the upper left corner. For the tag she used the template to cut a large tag from daisies paper, tore the bottom edge, matted it on solid blue and chalked the torn edge with blue chalk. She computer journaled on dot vellum then threaded three strands of floss through the eyelet. Arlene punched eight daisies, cut three petals from each then chalked them with tan and yellow chalk. She attached them using foam tape for dimension.

- **patterned Paper Pizazz™:** white leaves on blue, blue leaves on yellow, daisies, dot vellum (*Joy's Soft Collection of Papers*)
- **solid Paper Pizazz™:** light blue (*Soft Muted Tints*)
- **1½" wide sheer cream, ⅝" wide sheer blue ribbon:** Horizons Fabric, Inc.
- **1" daisy punch:** Family Treasures, Inc.
- **blue, tan, yellow decorating chalks:** Craf-T Products
- **light blue satin embroidery floss:** DMC
- **³⁄₁₆" gold eyelet:** Stamp Studio
- **tag template:** Paper Flair™ Tags Template
- **adhesive foam tape:** Therm O Web
- **designer:** Arlene Peterson

You fill our
Lives
with sunshine

Mom
&
Carol Lee

SPEED LIMIT 55

REST AREA

US 101

INTERSTATE 95

the open road

jim dukes july 2000

REST AREA

US 101

INTERSTATE 95

SPEED LIMIT 55

JIM & HIS BUDS ON THE DIRT BIKES

US 101

Janelle & David
With mom & dad
on our special day.

Stealing a kiss
before the reception

Schaber
wedding

the Bride

June 2, 200

Coordinating 2-Page Spreads

Scrapbook pages are rarely created one page at a time. Rather, we scrappers create double-page spreads, two pages that will face each other. And while a single layout is inspiring, many of us wonder, "So, what would I put on the facing page?"

In this chapter, you'll learn the tips for creating coordinating double-page spreads. How to coordinate by color, carry a theme throughout two pages, and tie accents and embellisments across a double-page spread are the three principles the Scrapbook Specialists use to create a two-page layout. The Scrapbook Specialists chose four of their favorite single-page layouts from this book, then created a second page as its companion.

Here's where you can learn to do the same. Learn the best designer tips and ideas for taking one great page idea and turning it into TWO fabulous pages!

1 Natalie's Easter was so special the day just wouldn't fit into one page—so, Paris created a second page! She chose the companion pink floral collage paper as a background for continuity. She used the same materials embellishing the first page, but changed the layout for a unique look.

6 Paris used a pink snap in each top corner to attach the vellum to the page.

2 Paris matted her photo on pink, leaving a $\frac{1}{16}$" border; then glued it as shown to a 6" white vellum square.

3 She placed the top portion of the vellum square on a cutting surface, then used the template and knife to cut five diamond folds. (These are the same folds used on the page below, but placed horizontally.) She glued each in place, then used the Scrappy Glue™ to adhere pink glitter on each folded diamond.

5 She wrapped the satin ribbon around the page bottom and glued the ends at the back, then glued an 11" length of sheer ribbon on top. She used the remaining ribbon to make a shoestring bow and attached it to the ribbon with a glue dot.

Grandma went a bit overboard with Natalie's Easter basket. It was full of candy, horse books and a huge stuffed rabbit! Can you tell she is the only granddaughter?

4 Paris computer journaled on a 7"x1⅞" rectangle of white vellum. She attached it to the page with a snap in each corner.

- **patterned Paper Pizazz™:** pink floral (8½"x11" *Collage Papers*)
- **specialty Paper Pizazz™:** white vellum (*Vellum Papers*, also by the sheet)
- **solid Paper Pizazz™:** pink (Plain Pastels)
- **Paper Flair™ templates:** Diamond Folds, Windows #2
- **¼" wide pink snaps:** Making Memories
- **11" of 1½" wide pink satin ribbon:** Offray Designer Ribbons™
- **27" of ⅝" wide pink sheer ribbon:** Sheer Creations
- **pink glitter, Scappy Glue™:** Magic Scraps
- **glue dots:** Glue Dots™ International LLC
- **X-acto® knife, cutting surface:** Hunt Mfg. Co.
- **black pen:** Zig® Writer
- **designer:** Paris Dukes

see "Easter 2002" on page 89

1 Toddi catered to this wedding party with a spectacular coordinating page. She used the same colors and materials, but changed the patterned paper background for a grand frame around the entire wedding party. The vertical flowers paper captures the greens and yellows of the first page, but adds magenta for a slightly different look. To make it easy, these papers are part of the same "family" in the book.

6 Toddi cut an inverted "V" into each end of the green ribbon, then scrunched the center and used a glue dot to adhere the ribbon rose as shown. She used one more glue dot to attach the ribbon to the page.

2 Toddi chose a black and white photo for a dramatic centerpiece.

5 She cut a 9½"x8" rectangle of yellow vellum, then placed it on a cutting surface. She used the knife to cut a 6"x5" window in the center of the vellum—that's larger than the photo, so the yellow is visable.

3 She matted the photo on an 8⅜"x7" rectangle of yellow paper, then tore along the bottom edge.

4 Toddi used the black pen to journal along the bottom edge of the photo mat.

Wedding Party

Schaber wedding

The Bride

June 2 2001

Team Joy

• **patterned Paper Pizazz™:** vertical flowers (*Mixing Heritage*)
• **specialty Paper Pizazz™:** pastel yellow vellum (*Pastel Vellum Papers*, also by the sheet)
• **solid Paper Pizazz™:** yellow (*Solid Muted Colors*)
• **¾" wide peach ribbon rose, 9" of 2" wide green satin ribbon:** C.M. Offray & Son, Inc.
• **black pen:** Sakura 5mm Micron
• **X-acto® knife, cutting surface:** Hunt Mfg. Co.
• **glue dots:** Glue Dots™ International LLC
• **designer:** Toddi Barclay

see "Team Joy" on page 61

1 Susan complimented a formal moment with an intimate one for these coordinating pages. She brought the rose patterned paper to the forefront to frame the romantic setting. Susan cut portions of the roses and leaves out with a knife to overlay onto the photo for an enchanting embellishment.

2 She began with a plaid background (which is part of the paper "family" in the book), then glued a 7½"x12" wide white vellum piece centered on top of a 9½"x12" pink vellum.

3 Susan cut a 6½"x12" rectangle of roses, then placed it on a cutting surface and used the knife to cut portions of the roses as shown.

4 She matted the rose rectangle on silver, leaving ⅛" border on each side.

7 Susan cut two 1" squares of foil, then cut each diagonally in half. She stenciled each triangle, then dabbed the pink pen onto a swab and into the stenciled areas.

6 She used the silver pen to journal on 2½"x1⅛" ivory, matted it on silver, then glued it centered on a 3⅛"x1" pink vellum rectangle, (just like the first family as done below).

Stealing a kiss before the reception

5 She matted the photo on white and silver, each with a ¹⁄₁₆" border, then tucked it under the cut out portions of the rose background paper.

- **patterned Paper Pizazz™:** pink roses, sage/pink plaid (*Joy's Vintage Papers*)
- **specialty Paper Pizazz™:** pink vellum (*Pastel Vellum Papers*, also by the sheet); white vellum (by the sheet); metallic silver (*Metallic Silver*, also by the sheet)
- **solid Paper Pizazz™:** ivory (*Plain Pastels*)
- **ArtEmboss™ light weight aluminum foil, wood embossing tool:** American Art Clay Co., Inc.
- **rose brass stencils:** American Traditions Stencils
- **pink pen:** Sakura Permapaque
- **silver pen:** Sakura Gelly Roll
- **rubbing alcohol, tissues, cotton swab**
- **computer mouse pad**
- **X-acto® knife, cutting surface:** Hunt Mfg. Co.
- **designer:** Susan Cobb

see *"Janelle & David"* on page 119

1 Paris followed the road signs to adventure for this thrilling coordinating page. She was inspired by the group shot to add more signs and action to this page, but used the same route for colors, road sign tags and tire tracks. Paris began with the road sign collage companion paper for the background.

6 Paris inserted eyelets and Twistel™ in two more tags to anchor the top left corner with the lower right.

2 She glued the photo to a 7½"x8" green vellum rectangle, then tore along the top and bottom edges.

5 She used the pen to journal on the vellum tag, punched a hole near the top and tied Twistel™ through the hole.

4 Paris matted a torn edge 6¾"x2" green vellum strip on a torn edge 7½"x3" white vellum strip, then inserted an eyelet near each end. She bent an 8" length of wire every ½" in a zigzag pattern and inserted the ends into the eyelets.

3 Paris inserted an eyelet into the top of each tag, then tied Twistel™ through each hole. She used a single layer of foam tape to attach the picnic tag and double layers for the US 101 sign.

JIM & HIS BUDS ON THE DIRT BIKES

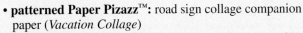

see "The Open Road" on page 64

- **patterned Paper Pizazz™**: road sign collage companion paper (*Vacation Collage*)
- **specialty Paper Pizazz™**: pastel green vellum (*Pastel Vellum Papers*, also by the sheet); white vellum (by the sheet)
- **road sign tags**: *Paper Pizazz™ Tag Art #2*
- **vellum tags, sage green Twistel™, 6 square pewter eyelets**: Making Memories™
- **dark green paper wrapped wire**: DMD Industries
- **glue dots**: Glue Dots™ International LLC
- **foam adhesive tape**: Therm O Web
- **black pen**: Zebra Jimnie Gel Rollerball
- **designer**: Paris Dukes

You have given me the greatest gift of all... a family.

H is for his sense of HUMOR

Ever since he was a little boy, Matt has always had a great (sometimes downright wicked) sense of humor. He shared this talent with others as a cartoonist for the Eugene Register Guard's 20Below section.

Wit has truth in it; wisecracking is simply calisthenics with words. —Dorothy Parker

CARTOONIST
Matt Villanueva

School: Churchill International High School
Year: Freshman
The word I hate most: "Solicitors." They mispronounce my last name.
The word I love most: "Hedgehog," because I own one.
Strangest thing about me: My ability to do other people's voices (Dr. Evil, Cartman, Austin Powers, Jack Nicholson)
Band I'd have play at my own personal concert: Save Ferris
Person I'd like to sit around a campfire with: John Belushi
If I could star in any TV show, it would be: "The Simpsons"
The world would be a better place if: Teen-agers were better respected in society. Not all teens are going to rip off a store. At least 86 percent of us are decent human beings.

a small slice of life / Matt Villanueva...

Gift Albums

For whom do you scrapbook? If you're like many of us, you create albums to celebrate special memories for those you love. Maybe those people are your children, your husband or partner, or other members of your family. You might also create scrapbooks that honor those who touch your life—a child's teacher, perhaps, a coach or a good friend.

This is truly simple scrapbooking at its best! There's no need to scrapbook every photo. The album can be as long or short as you wish. Your journaling can feature heartfelt remembrances or simple recipes. Best of all, you'll be giving someone a gift that no money can buy— your time, your creativity and your love.

Here you'll find many kinds of gift albums created by the Scrapbook Specialists. From a celebration of a child's name to a collection of family recipes, we've got ideas for great gift books. You'll also find clever, creative ways to cover albums so you can personalize your book, too.

As you read this chapter, we think you'll agree a scrapbook is a heartfelt way to celebrate your creativity while gifting a special person with your time and love.

roses, stripes papers from *Paper Pizazz*™ *Soft Florals & Patterns*

Gift albums are to scrapbooking what frames are to paintings—they enclose your works of art. Sara created Molly Rose's gift album is an artful combination of scrapbook pages and journaling to detail her niece's life. She chose Molly's favorite colors and themes to highlight her niece's personality. To make it all work, Sara used the letters in Molly's name to tell the story of her niece. What a perfect gift!

Sara began Molly's gift album with a simple, yet sophisticated title page. She used pink rose patterned paper for a background, then glued a pink striped rectangle, matted on white on top. Sara chose a fun font, then computered journaled on pink vellum and tore the edges for a softened look. A pretty sheer ribbon bow and eyelets completed the page.

Molly's name inspired Sara to use a tag to feature each letter. She formed little cards of words detailing her niece's traits, which were computer journaled on solid ivory paper using one font for uniformity. Each card was matted on pink vellum and attached to the page with a single pink eyelet. A pink brushstrokes patterned paper was used for a subtle background.

The right side page featured a large photo, matted on ivory paper, then on pink vellum with torn edges. Below the photo, a single ivory card is placed to complete the spread. A pink dots background paper compliments the left page paper.

pink brushstrokes paper from *Paper Pizazz*™ *Light Great Backgrounds*

pink dots paper from *Paper Pizazz*™ *Soft Tints*

Sara matted Molly's photo in multiple layers of pinks and yellows for interest. She began with a pink/yellow gingham patterned background. She continued the tag theme with the next letter from Molly's name and its meaning, both on solid ivory and matted on pink paper. A fun twist of metallic pink fiber was added to the tag.

pink/yellow gingham, yellow squiggles papers from *Paper Pizazz™ Soft Tints*

O *is for ORIGINAL*

L *is also for LOVED*

Mom

Molly is well-loved by so many people...

blue posies, blue moiré papers from *Paper Pizazz™ Soft Tints*

Dad

Mommy Lisa & Papa Ken

Aunt Belinda & Uncle Owl

Bug & Bob

Aunt Sara & Uncle Keith

Cousin Matt

Uncle T & Uncle Bi

Cousin Ashley

Michelle

blue dots paper from *Paper Pizazz™ Lisa Williams Blue, Yellow & Green*

Molly's blue dress was reason to change the color scheme on this fun 2-page spread. The ivory paper tag and cards featured the same fonts for consistency, though these were matted on blue vellum to complement the blue floral and dots patterned background papers. Yes, there was another double-page "L" theme which focused on "little girl".

Y *is for all that's YET to be!*

Soft yellows kept the soft feel of the album, yet were bright enough for a backdrop of the vivid red in Molly's pretty shirt. The tag and card featured the same fonts, with a metallic fiber topping it off.

- **pink, yellow vellums:** *Paper Pizazz™ Pastel Vellum Papers*
- **tag template:** *Paper Flair™ Tags Template*
- **fibers:** Adornaments™
- **ribbon:** C.M. Offray & Son, Inc.
- **eyelets:** Stamp Studio
- **designer:** Sara Naumann

yellow dots, yellow gingham paper from *Paper Pizazz™ Soft Tints*

Matthew:
A Gift From God

Joseph:
God Will Increase

blue tri-dots paper from *Paper Pizazz*™
Dots, Checks, Plaids & Stripes

Sara created a fun theme for Matthew's album which reflects his personality as he grew. She matted each photo on bright white, a wider striking red and another layer of white for a dramatic effect. She reversed the color scheme for the journaling.

The blue patterned background papers provide a cool contrast to the vivid reds in the photos and mats. The gold star snaps in the name box add a perfect touch to the page.

Mom Says:

Matthew: because it means 'gift from God' ~ and we didn't want to give Uncle John the satisfaction of calling you Duncan.

Dad Says:

Joseph: Named after Grampa V,
Joseph Humberto

blue plaid paper from *Paper Pizazz*™ *Dots, Checks, Plaids & Stripes*

The color scheme was repeated for the next spread, but with an entirely different look!

Sara chose a clean font for journaling to be easy to read and to complement the simple, yet striking color theme. Each letter is placed on a matted tag, then attached to the page with a red eyelet. Sara thread red fiber through the eyelets for a fun border to balance the two-page spread.

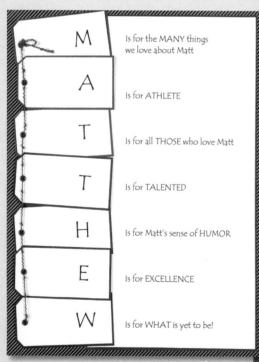

M Is for the MANY things we love about Matt

A Is for ATHLETE

T Is for all THOSE who love Matt

T Is for TALENTED

H Is for Matt's sense of HUMOR

E Is for EXCELLENCE

W Is for WHAT is yet to be!

blue diagonal stripes, white stars on red papers from *Paper Pizazz*™ *Dots, Checks, Plaids & Stripes*

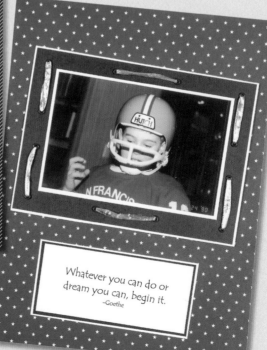

Whatever you can do or dream you can, begin it.
-Goethe

Sara tackled a bit more to give Matthew's photo more punch. She repeated the double mat theme, then inserted red eyelets along the blue layer. She thread white fiber through the eyelets. Foam tape was used to adhere the photo to the page.

H is for his sense of HUMOR

Ever since he was a little boy, Matt has always had a great (sometimes downright wicked) sense of humor. He shared this talent with others as a cartoonist for the Eugene Register Guard's 20Below section.

blue/green stripes paper from *Paper Pizazz™ Bright Great Backgrounds*

Personality is key to making an album a true gift—so, let your subject's personality shine through! Sara used pictures, stories and other memorabilia to show Matthew's characteristics. She used fun neon stripes as a background to his funny face, then chose a more subtle pattern as a backdrop for a variety of elements on the facing page. Matting each piece on matching blue paper presents a clean look, yet ties everything together. It works beautifully.

Wit has truth in it; wisecracking is simply calisthenics with words. –Dorothy Parker

blue brushstrokes paper from *Paper Pizazz™ Bright Great Backgrounds*

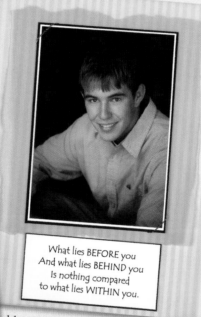

W is for WHAT is yet to be!

What lies BEFORE you
And what lies BEHIND you
Is nothing compared
to what lies WITHIN you.

blue stripes paper from *Paper Pizazz™ Soft Tints*

blue "handmade" paper from *Paper Pizazz™ "Handmade" Papers*

To highlight Matthew's growing sophistication, Sara created sophisticated layouts. She used black, white and silver papers to mat Matthew's photo. She matted the white letter tag and journaling on a single layer of black for a striking look. The right page features the same matting theme, upon a torn edge blue vellum rectangle to soften the striking effect of the blacks and whites. Metallic thread was wrapped around two corners for subtle sparkle.

A gift for
Matthew Joseph
from his
Aunt Sara and Uncle Keith
Christmas 2001

Even the last page is important in a gift album—think of it as the wrapping and bow on a package. Sara created an elegant effect using metallic gold paper, eyelets and photo corners to surround her final page. She matted a scuffed brown patterned paper onto tan and brown for a rich look, then highlighted the edges with the photo corners. She printed her message, matted it on tan, then used a gold eyelet at the top corners to attach it to a metallic gold quilted patterned paper, also matted on tan. What a spectacular finish for a sensational book!

scuffed brown paper from *Paper Pizazz™ Spattered, Crackled & Sponged;* gold quilt paper from *Paper Flair™ Gold & Ivory*

- **metallic silver paper:** *Paper Pizazz™ Metallic Silver,* also by the sheet
- **tag template:** *Paper Flair™ Tags Template*
- **star snaps:** AmericanPin/Hyglo®
- **designer:** Sara Naumann
- **eyelets:** Stamp Studio
- **fibers:** Adornments™

Bon Bon Peppermint Pie

Shauna created a great way to give her pie recipe as a gift. She covered peppermints with white vellum, then placed a torn strip of cookies with white eyelets and a ribbon as shown. She printed the lists each on white, then matted each on red and cookies papers. She inserted an eyelet and ribbon into the ingredients card and red buttons with floss on the directions. Shauna stitched a vellum pocket onto the page and inserted the ingredients list. She wrapped ribbon through the top eyelets and used the remaining for a bow. For the candy: she drew red stripes on the pebble, wrapped it in vellum and used a glue dot to attach it to the bow. Yummy!

- **patterned Paper Pizazz™:** peppermints, chocolate sandwich cookies (*Yummy Papers*)
- **specialty Paper Pizazz™:** 2 sheets of white vellum (by the sheet)
- **solid Paper Pizazz™:** red (*Plain Brights*); white (*Plain Pastels*)
- **³⁄₁₆" wide white eyelets:** Stamp Studio
- **32" of ⁵⁄₈" wide red gingham sheer ribbon, ¼" wide red buttons, ¾" wide opaque white picture pebble:** Magic Scraps™
- **white embroidery floss:** DMC
- **red, black pens:** Sakura Permapaque
- **glue dots:** Glue Dots™ International LLC
- **sewing needle**
- **designer:** Shauna Berglund-Immel

This introduction page to a recipe album was easy to prepare. Shauna used a blue handpainted paper for a background, then cut individual cookies, glued some to the page and attached others with foam tape. She printed the dedication and table of contents on white rectangles, and matted each on red. Then she glued each to a 5¼"x4½" white rectangle, cut the top to form an index tab and used the pen to print the tab subject. She repeated the process with the photo. What a fun gift to share with others!

- **patterned Paper Pizazz™:** blue handpainted with white/red checks border (*BJ's Handpainted Papers*); chocolate chip cookies (*Childhood Memories*, also by the sheet)
- **solid Paper Pizazz™:** red (*Solid Jewel Tones*); white (*Plain Pastels*)
- **foam adhesive tape:** Therm O Web
- **black pen:** Sakura Gelly Roll
- **designer:** Shauna Berglund-Immel

Oatmeal Chocolate Chip Cookies

Shauna baked up this great idea with tan vellum over crackle paper, then tore the left edge of a 3" chocolate chips strip. She layered tan vellum over a 1" crackle strip then matted it on black. She printed the ingredients and directions on white and matted each on black. She used the template to make three crackle/tan vellum tags, then inserted a large eyelet with fibers as shown. She filled the pockets with beads, oatmeal and glitter then glued each to a tag. Smaller tags were attached to each. I'm hungry!

- **patterned Paper Pizazz™:** chocolate chips (*Yummy Papers*); 2 sheets of crackle (by the sheet)
- **specialty Paper Pizazz™:** 2 sheets of tan vellum (*Pastel Vellum Papers*, also by the sheet)
- **solid Paper Pizazz™:** white (*Plain Pastels*); black (*Solid Jewel Tones*)
- **⅛", ³⁄₁₆" copper eyelets:** Stamp Studio
- **tags:** *Paper Flair™ Tags Template*
- **beige fibers:** Adornaments™
- **tan seed beads:** Blue Moon Beads/ Elizabeth Ward & Co., Inc.
- **white glitter:** Magic Scraps™
- **2" wide clear memorabilia pockets, foam adhesive tape:** Therm O Web
- **oatmeal**
- **brown pen:** Zig® Scroll
- **black pen:** Sakura Gelly Roll
- **designer:** Shauna Berglund-Immel

An apple a day may work for some teachers, but a gift album makes the grade for that special teacher! Plus, it's a gift the entire class can create. Shauna and the other parents worked with the students to create a fun layout and gather all the items together. She chose alpha beads to decorate Mrs. Becker's page.

Background papers set the tone for the page. Shauna chose primary colors to reflect those used in Spencer and Natalie's first grade classroom. The simple patterns on bold colors make for fun pages, yet allow for individuality. The red mesh paper on Mrs. Becker's page works well with the schoolhouse Punch-Out™. Shauna chose green mesh for the mascot page and used gingham prints for the student pages.

Continuity was key to building a gift album. Shauna used white for each photo mat as one recurring theme in the album. The color mat matches one from the page, as Shanua showed using yellow for the first layer on Mrs. Becker's photo mat. School photos of each student were used to add to the academic look of the album. Tags also played an important role in the album. Shauna used paper tags for each student to write a special message, then tied satin ribbons onto each. She chose more elaborate tags for the mascot page and wrapped them in a pretty bronze sheer ribbon.

Details of each student made this album a keeper! Shauna passed out tags to each student and asked them to write what makes Mrs. Becker special on one tag and their favorite classes on the other. For fun, each student chose their favorite stickers from the Annie Lang collections to embellish their tags and name plate. The stickers add whimsy and color to the tags and allow each student to reflect a bit of their personality onto the page. No wonder the album made honor roll!

- **patterned Paper Pizazz™**: red mesh, green mesh, yellow gingham, blue gingham, green gingham, pink swirls (*Bright Tints*)
- **solid Paper Pizazz™**: yellow, tan (*Solid Muted Colors*); red (*Plain Brights*); white (*Plain Pastels*)
- **Paper Pizazz™ stickers:** Annie Lang's School Time, Annie Lang's Little Boys #2
- **schoolhouse:** *Paper Pizazz™ Clever Frames Punch-Outs™*
- **tags:** *Paper Flair™ Tags Template*
- **alpha beads:** Darice
- **apples, scissors, tree, paw, dogbone buttons:** Dress It Up
- **24-gauge gold wire:** Colour Craft™
- **⅛" wide white eyelets:** Stamp Studio
- **metal rim circle tags:** Making Memories
- **¼" wide red, pink, blue satin ribbon:** C.M. Offray & Son, Inc.
- **⅞" wide bronze sheer ribbon:** MSI Sheer Creations
- **black, blue, red pens:** Zig® Writer
- **designers:** Shauna Berglund-Immel, Spencer Immel, Natalie Dukes

Shauna used 10 themes to highlight the 10 ways she loves her husband in this romantic gift album. Each section includes two 7"x5" coordinating pages featuring one element of her feelings. The first page introduced the reason and the second provided a pictorial example. Reason #8 used a winning combination of brown/tan diamonds and plaid patterned papers. Shauna matted a diamonds piece on dark brown for each page. She computer journaled on white, matted on brown, then overlapped a small matted photo. Shauna matted ½" wide plaid strips on brown, then white and wrapped one around opposing corners as shown. She repeated the theme with 1" plaid squares then used foam tape to attach each to a corner strip. Shauna tied floss in each button then glued one to each square. She inserted a silver eyelet into a round paper tag then tied floss through the eyelet onto the button as shown.

Reason #9 includes each of their children. Shauna used blue plaid, matted on black for both backgrounds. She layered ½" wide blue stripes onto a 2" blue gingham for the left side of the first page, tearing along the right edges. Shauna matted a coordinating blue gingham tag on white, then used the black pen to journal inside the solid center of the tag. She attached it to the page with an eyelet and fiber at the top. She reversed the side border effect for the second page, then inserted a white eyelet near the top and bottom as shown. She inserted an eyelet onto a round tag, threaded fiber through the eyelet then inserted the fiber ends into the eyelets.

The end is black and white—and striking! Shauna matted gray plaid on black for each background. She layered strips of tiles and stripes with top torn edges onto the first, then placed her journaling centered on the page. She wrapped black ribbon around the bottom and used an 8" length to tie a bow. Shauna glued a 3½"x5" black stripes on the right side of the second page then glued the family portrait, matted on white and black, in the center. She wrapped silver ribbon around the right side. She inserted a silver eyelet into a round vellum tag then used floss to tie it onto the silver bow as shown.

- **patterned Paper Pizazz™**: brown/tan diamonds, brown/tan plaid, gray plaid, black stripes, gray tiles, blue stripes, blue plaid, blue gingham (*Mixing Masculine Papers*)
- **solid Paper Pizazz™**: dark brown, dark blue, black (*Solid Jewel Tones*); white (*Plain Pastels*)
- **blue tag**: *Paper Pizazz™ Tag Art #2*
- ³⁄₁₆" white, ⅛" wide silver eyelets: Stamp Studio
- **small vellum, paper metal rimmed round tags**: Making Memories
- ⅝" wide silver, black sheer ribbon: C.M. Offray & Son, Inc.
- **blue fibers**: Adornaments™
- **ivory embroidery floss**: DMC
- **glue dots**: Glue Dots™ Intl. LLC
- **foam adhesive tape**: Therm O Web
- **black pen**: Sakura Gelly Roll
- **designer**: Shauna Berglund-Immel

Y ou can judge an album by its cover—if it's handmade by LeNae! She chose vintage blues for the background papers, using a 6"x10½" monochromatic floral on the left and stripes on the right of each cardboard piece. LeNae wrapped the paper edges to the back and glued them. A 9½"x8½" of ivory was glued to the back to conceal the patterned paper ends. She glued a torn 7¾"x7" white vellum centered on the front. She matted a 6" blue floral square on white, turned it on point and glued it centered on the front. LeNae glued a torn edge 6"x4½" blue vellum on the diamond. She cut out the blue floral tag, punched a hole at the top then tied blue and white fibers through the hole. She glued it to the blue vellum at an angle. She glued two leaves on each side of the tag, then used the pen to personalize the tag. LeNae placed the insides together, with the stripes on the right. She used the setter and hammer to make nine holes evenly spaced along the left side then inserted brads into the holes.

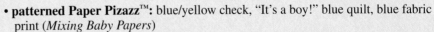
The brads allow you to insert as many pages inside as you need!

- **patterned Paper Pizazz**™: blue floral, blue stripes, blue monochromatic floral (*Joy's Vintage Papers*)
- **specialty Paper Pizazz**™: white vellum (*Vellum Papers*, also by the sheet); dark blue vellum (*Pastel Vellum Papers*)
- **solid Paper Pizazz**™: light ivory, white (*Plain Pastels*)
- **tags:** *Paper Pizazz*™ *Tag Art #2*
- **two 9"x10" sheets of medium weight cardboard**

- **⅜" wide white capped brads:** AmericanPin/Hyglo®
- **2" navy blue skeleton leaves:** Black Ink
- **blue, white fibers:** Adornaments™
- **¼" wide circle punch:** Family Treasures, Inc.
- **eyelet setter, hammer**
- **metallic blue pen:** Sakura Gelly Roll
- **designer:** LeNae Gerig

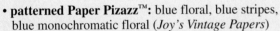

T he excitement and joy of your precious arrival is a most special occasion. LeNae created an adorable mini-album for such a grand announcement. She covered each cardboard piece with blue fabric paper. She matted a 3¾"x6" of checks onto solid yellow and glued it centered on the front of one covered cardboard. She glued a 3¼" blue quilt square, matted on white near the bottom as shown. For the inside, she cut one 11¼"x6" and two 8"x6" yellow rectangles. She scored 3¾" from the left edge of the 11¼" piece, then twice more, 3¾" apart. She repeated for each 8" rectangle. She glued the pieces together using the extra ½" on the right sides to create a seven-panel accordian fold. LeNae glued the first panel to the back of the front cover and the last panel to the inside of the back cover. She cut alphabet tiles spelling the baby's name then cut out the teddy bear and glued the pieces as shown, using foam tape. She wrapped the ribbon around the album and tie the ends in a bow.

- **patterned Paper Pizazz**™: blue/yellow check, "It's a boy!" blue quilt, blue fabric print (*Mixing Baby Papers*)
- **solid Paper Pizazz**™: white (*Plain Pastels*); 2 sheets of yellow (*12"x12" Solid Pastel Papers*)
- **letter tiles:** *Artsy Collage*™ *Alphabet Tiles*
- **bear:** *Paper Pizazz*™ *Stack 'em Cut-Outs*™
- **two 4"x6¼" sheets of medium weight cardboard**
- **18" of 1½" wide white sheer ribbon:** C.M. Offray & Son, Inc.
- **foam adhesive tape:** Therm O Web
- **designer:** LeNae Gerig

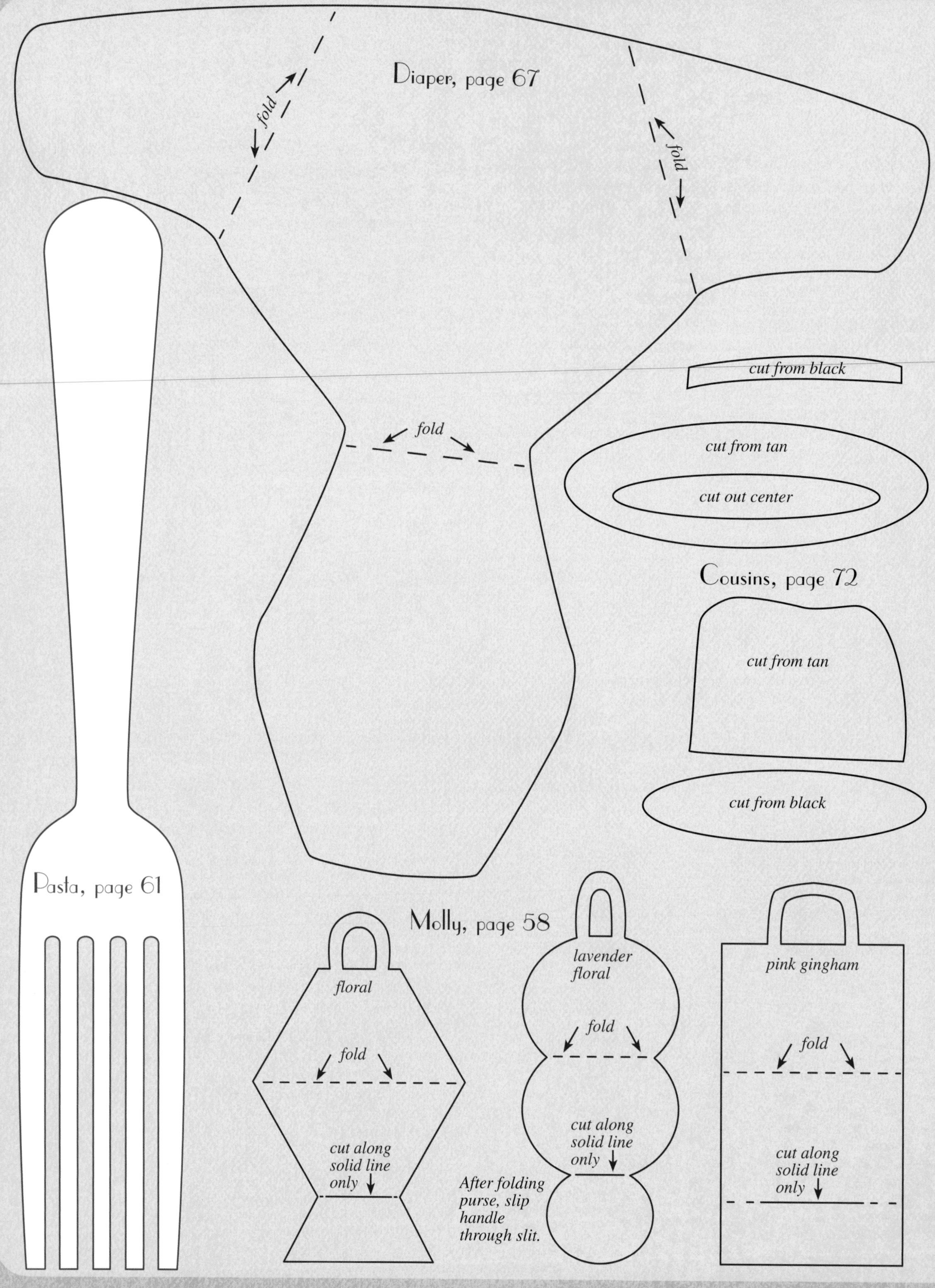

Diaper, page 67

fold

fold

fold

cut from black

cut from tan

cut out center

Cousins, page 72

cut from tan

cut from black

Pasta, page 61

Molly, page 58

floral

fold

cut along
solid line
only ↓

*lavender
floral*

fold

cut along
solid line
only ↓

*After folding
purse, slip
handle
through slit.*

pink gingham

fold

cut along
solid line
only ↓

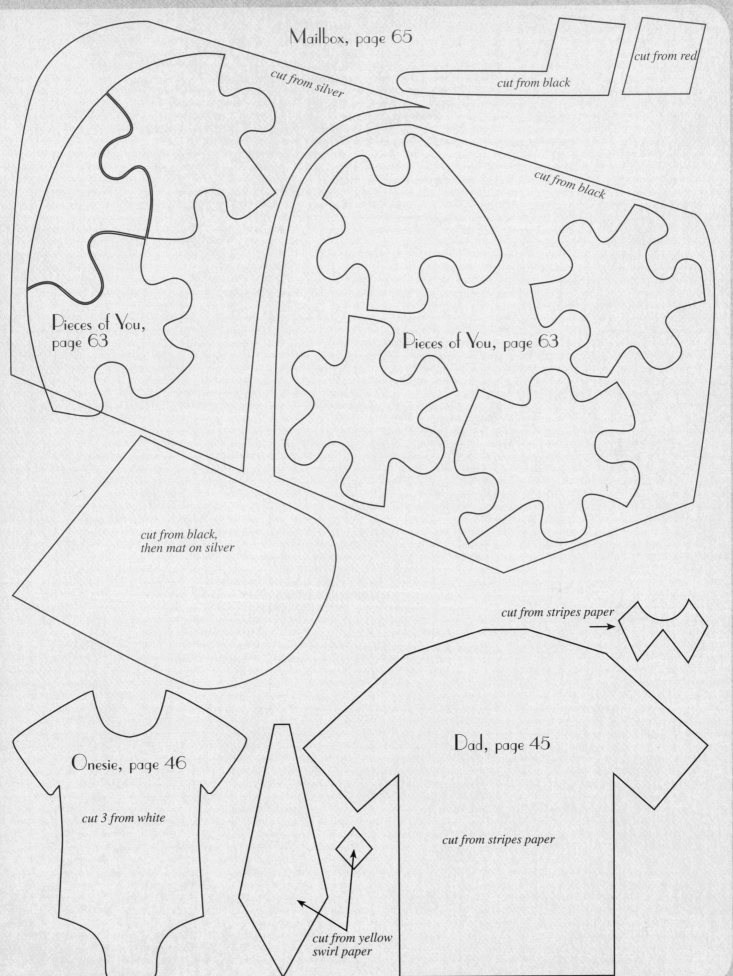

Mailbox, page 65

cut from silver

cut from black

cut from red

cut from black

Pieces of You,
page 63

Pieces of You, page 63

cut from black,
then mat on silver

cut from stripes paper

Dad, page 45

Onesie, page 46

cut 3 from white

cut from stripes paper

cut from yellow
swirl paper

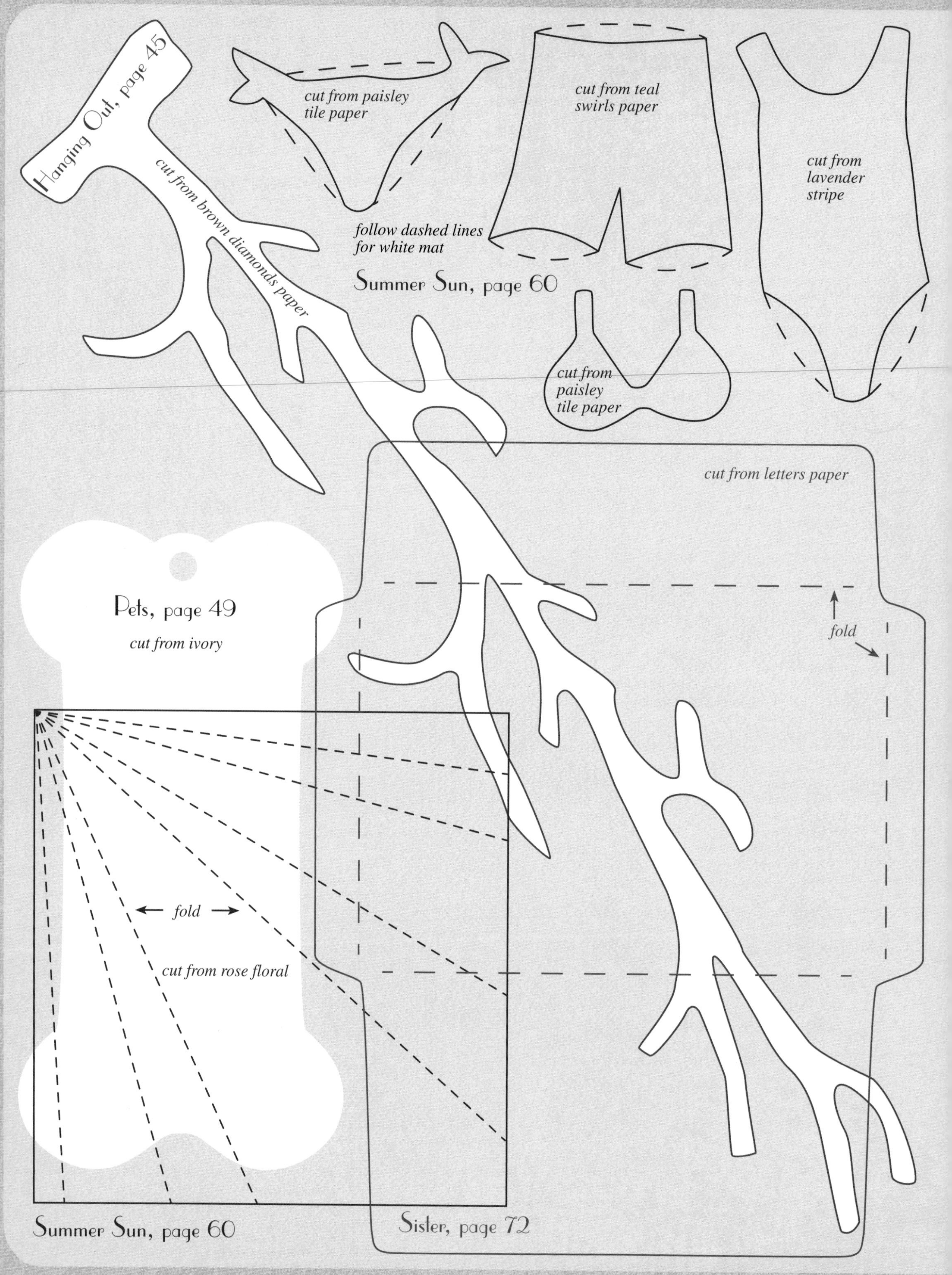

Hanging Out, page 45

cut from brown diamonds paper

cut from paisley tile paper

follow dashed lines for white mat

Summer Sun, page 60

cut from teal swirls paper

cut from lavender stripe

cut from paisley tile paper

cut from letters paper

fold

Pets, page 49

cut from ivory

fold

cut from rose floral

Summer Sun, page 60

Sister, page 72

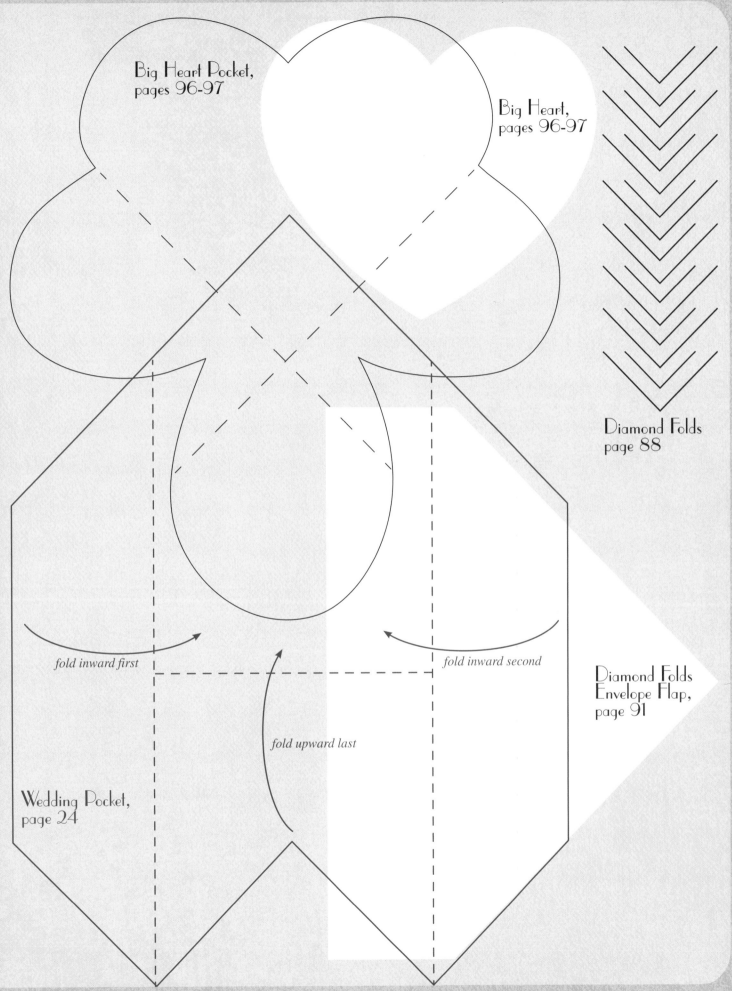

Big Heart Pocket,
pages 96-97

Big Heart,
pages 96-97

Diamond Folds
page 88

fold inward first

fold inward second

Diamond Folds
Envelope Flap,
page 91

fold upward last

Wedding Pocket,
page 24

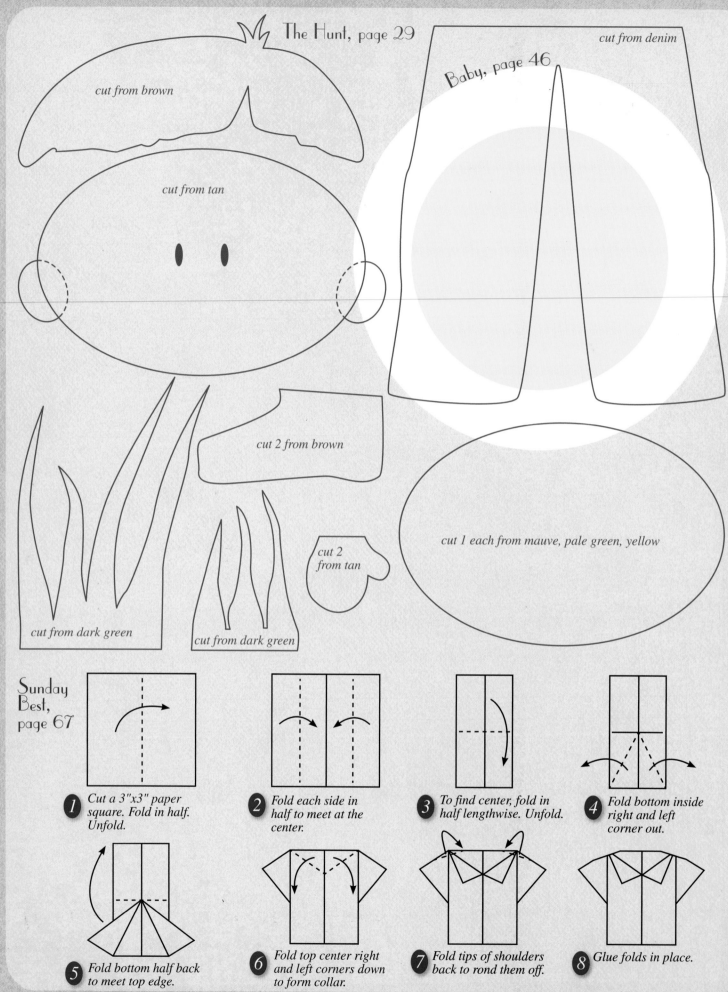

The Hunt, page 29

cut from brown

cut from denim

Baby, page 46

cut from tan

cut 2 from brown

cut 1 each from mauve, pale green, yellow

cut 2 from tan

cut from dark green

cut from dark green

Sunday Best, page 67

1 Cut a 3"x3" paper square. Fold in half. Unfold.

2 Fold each side in half to meet at the center.

3 To find center, fold in half lengthwise. Unfold.

4 Fold bottom inside right and left corner out.

5 Fold bottom half back to meet top edge.

6 Fold top center right and left corners down to form collar.

7 Fold tips of shoulders back to rond them off.

8 Glue folds in place.